P9-DTX-304

GREAT ARTISTS OF THE WESTERN WORLD

The Baroque Tradition

The Baroque Tradition

Caravaggio

Diego Velázquez

Anthony Van Dyck

Jacob van Ruisdael

MARSHALL CAVENDISH · LONDON · NEW YORK · SYDNEY

Staff Credits

Editors — *Clive Gregory LLB*
Sue Lyon BA (Honours)

Art Editors — *Chris Legee BFA*
Kate Sprawson BA (Honours)
Keith Vollans LSIAD

Deputy Editor — *John Kirkwood BSc (Honours)*

Sub-editors — *Caroline Bugler BA (Honours), MA*
Sue Churchill BA (Honours)
Alison Cole BA, MPhil
Jenny Mohammadi
Nigel Rodgers BA (Honours), MA
Penny Smith
Will Steeds BA (Honours), MA

Designers — *Stuart John*
Julie Stanniland

Picture Researchers — *Vanessa Fletcher BA (Honours)*
Flavia Howard BA (Honours)
Jessica Johnson BA

Production Controllers — *Tom Helsby*
Alan Stewart BSc

Secretary — *Lynn Smail*

Editorial Director — *Maggi McCormick*

Publishing Manager — *Robert Paulley BSc*

Managing Editor — *Alan Ross BA (Honours)*

Consultant and Authenticator — *Sharon Fermor BA (Honours) Lecturer in the Extra-Mural Department of London University and Lecturer in Art History at Sussex University*

Reference Edition Published 1988

Published by Marshall Cavendish Corporation
147 West Merrick Road
Freeport, Long Island
N.Y. 11520

Typeset by Litho Link Ltd., Welshpool
Printed and Bound by Dai Nippon
Printing Co., Hong Kong Ltd.

Library of Congress Cataloging-in-Publication Data

Main entry under title:

Great Artists of the Western World II.

Includes index.
1. Artists – Biography. I. Marshall Cavendish Corporation.
N40.G774 1988 709'.2'2 [B] 88–4317
ISBN 0–86307–900–8 (set)

ISBN 0–86307–900–8 (set)
0–86307–756–0 (vol)

Preface

Looking at pictures can be one of the greatest pleasures that life has to offer. Note, however, those two words 'can be'; all too many of us remember all too clearly those grim afternoons of childhood when we were dragged, bored to tears and complaining bitterly, through room after room of Italian primitives by well-meaning relations or tight-lipped teachers. It was enough to put one off pictures for life – which, for some of us, was exactly what it did.

For if gallery-going is to be the fun it should be, certain conditions must be fulfilled. First, the pictures we are to see must be good pictures. Not necessarily great *pictures – even a few of these can be daunting, while too many at a time may prove dangerously indigestible. But they must be well-painted, by good artists who know precisely both the effect they want to achieve and how best to achieve it. Second, we must limit ourselves as to quantity. Three rooms – four at the most – of the average gallery are more than enough for one day, and for best results we should always leave while we are still fresh, well before satiety sets in. Now I am well aware that this is a counsel of perfection: sometimes, in the case of a visiting exhibition or, perhaps, when we are in a foreign city with only a day to spare, we shall have no choice but to grit our teeth and stagger on to the end. But we shall not enjoy ourselves quite so much, nor will the pictures remain so long or so clearly in our memory.*

The third condition is all-important: we must know something about the painters whose work we are looking at. And this is where this magnificent series of volumes – one of which you now hold in your hands – can make all the difference. No painting is an island: it must, if it is to be worth a moment's attention, express something of the personality of its painter. And that painter, however individual a genius, cannot but reflect the country, style and period, together with the views and attitudes of the people among whom he or she was born and bred. Even a superficial understanding of these things will illuminate a painting for us far better than any number of spotlights, and if in addition we have learnt something about the artist as a person – life and loves, character and beliefs, friends and patrons, and the places to which he or she travelled – the interest and pleasure that the work will give us will be multiplied a hundredfold.

Great Artists of the Western World *will provide you with just such an insight into the life and work of some of the outstanding painters of Europe and America. The text is informative without ever becoming dry or academic, not limiting itself to the usual potted biographies but forever branching out into the contemporary world outside and beyond workshop or studio. The illustrations, in colour throughout, have been dispensed in almost reckless profusion. For those who, like me, revel in playing the Attribution Game – the object of which is to guess the painter of each picture before allowing one's eye to drop to the label – the little sections on 'Trademarks' are a particularly happy feature; but every* aficionado *will have particular preferences, and I doubt whether there is an art historian alive, however distinguished, who would not find some fascinating nugget of previously unknown information among the pages that follow.*

This series, however, is not intended for art historians. It is designed for ordinary people like you and me – and for our older children – who are fully aware that the art galleries of the world constitute a virtually bottomless mine of potential enjoyment, and who are determined to extract as much benefit and advantage from it as they possibly can. All the volumes in this collection will enable us to do just that, expanding our knowledge not only of art itself but also of history, religion, mythology, philosophy, fashion, interior decoration, social customs and a thousand other subjects as well. So let us not simply leave them around, flipping idly through a few of their pages once in a while. Let us read them as they deserve to be read – and welcome a new dimension in our lives.

John Julius Norwich

John Julius Norwich is a writer and broadcaster who has written histories of Venice and of Norman Sicily as well as several works on history, art and architecture. He has also made over twenty documentary films for television, including the recent **Treasure Houses of Britain** ***series which was widely acclaimed after repeated showings in the United States.***

Lord Norwich is Chairman of the Venice in Peril Fund, and member of the Executive Committee of the British National Trust, an independently funded body established for the protection of places of historic interest and natural beauty.

Contents

Introduction — 8
The Baroque and baroque – fierce realism – sympathy and insight – portraits at court – lyrical landscapes

Caravaggio — 11

The Artist's Life — 12
Life in Rome – an influential patron – ambitious paintings – criminal exploits – exile and death

The Artist at Work — 18
Fierce originality – truth to nature – chiaroscuro – provocative images – making of a masterpiece

Gallery — 24
Religious paintings of astonishing realism

In the Background: The Caravaggisti — 36
Influence of the Master – followers in Naples – the movement in Holland – Georges de La Tour

A Year in the Life: 1600 — 40
The Earl of Essex – war in Holland – rebels in Scotland

Diego Velázquez — 43

The Artist's Life — 44
Birth in Seville – sympathetic teacher – royal favour – a visit to Italy – 'mourned by all'

The Artist at Work — 50
Early assurance – a change of direction – essential humanity – an eye for truth – making of a masterpiece

Gallery — 56
Court portraits and a famous nude

In the Background: Philip IV — 68
An empire in decline – a weak king and a powerful minister – royal extravagance – ebbing power

A Year in the Life: 1656 — 72
Civil war in France – the rule of Oliver Cromwell

Anthony Van Dyck — 75

The Artist's Life — 76
Early life in Antwerp – success and fame – life in Italy – King's Painter in England – marriage and death

The Artist at Work — 82
The influence of Italy – equestrian portraits – aristocratic images – making of a masterpiece

Gallery — 88
Early religious paintings and court portraits

In the Background: Charles I — 100
The Prince of Wales – friction with Parliament – an unpopular French wife – the drift to civil war

A Year in the Life: 1635 — 104
Ship Money – war between France and Spain – the Académie Française

Jacob van Ruisdael — 107

The Artist's Life — 108
The city of Haarlem – an early influence – artistic connections – a talented family – life in Amsterdam

The Artist at Work — 112
Revolutionary landscapes – creative approach – a master draughtsman – making of a masterpiece

Gallery — 120
Landscapes of drama and power

In the Background: The Age of Observation — 132
Dutch independence – the scientific revolution – the importance of trade

A Year in the Life: 1648 — 136
The Peace of Westphalia – victory at Lens – second civil war in England

Appendix — 139

Gallery Guide — 139
Where to see the works of Caravaggio, Velàzquez, Van Dyck and Ruisdael

Bibliography — 139

Other Baroque Artists — 140
From Gianlorenzo Bernini to Franciso Zurburan – lives and major works of other artists of the Baroque tradition

Index — 142

Introduction

The Baroque age provides one of the most attractive and diversified interludes in the history of art. The word itself is used in two quite distinct senses. In precise terms, Baroque relates to the vigorous and exuberant style that revitalized Western art when the creative energies that were summoned up by the Renaissance were becoming exhausted. There is, however, a more general, secondary usage. Many commentators employ 'baroque' (with a small 'b') as a blanket term for the art of the 17th century. This can cause confusion, since the same century also witnessed the rise of Classicism and there was a considerable degree of overlap between the two styles. To cite a single instance, the work of Georges de La Tour (see p.39) displays the strong lighting contrasts that derived from Caravaggio and the Baroque, while his figures have the serenity that is normally associated with Classical art.

The word 'Baroque' originated from the Portuguese barroco, meaning a misshapen pearl, and was used scornfully by those who saw the movement as a decadent tail-piece to the Renaissance. These derogatory overtones persisted to some extent until the 19th century, fuelled by critics such as John Ruskin, but the positive values of the style are now fully recognized.

The birthplace of the Baroque was in Rome, where it was carefully nurtured by the papacy. The Catholic Church, reeling under the advances made by the Protestants during the early 16th century, launched its own drive to regain the spiritual leadership of Europe – the Counter-Reformation – at the Council of Trent in 1563.

Initially, this involved a massive re-building programme in Rome itself, aimed at reasserting the city's position as the spiritual capital of the world. Painters, too, were to benefit from this papal initiative; in addition to the extra commissions which arose out of the new building work, the church issued guidelines offering new goals for which artists were to strive. Modern religious art, it was suggested, should be clear and intelligible; should be realistic enough to enable spectators to identify readily with the subjects; and should have a powerful emotional appeal. No one fulfilled these three requirements better than Caravaggio.

Fierce Realism

In Caravaggio's Biblical pictures, nothing was more striking than the sheer physicality of the events portrayed. The features of his Abraham or St Peter (pp.26 and 31) were as gross and plebeian as those of a shepherd or an executioner, and Caravaggio revelled in the depiction of such unglamorous details as chunky, muscular legs and muddied feet. In addition, his paintings abounded with dramatic gestures and movements that were as ungainly as they were brilliantly observed. These elements provided a stark contrast to the statuesque calm and beauty of most Renaissance models and to the artificial elegance and elongated figures of the succeeding Mannerist painters.

Most contemporaries found Caravaggio's inventions compelling rather than shocking. Much has been made of his turbulent lifestyle and some critics have sought to link this with the occasional rejection of his work. However, Caravaggio was never short of patrons. His Death of the Virgin, for example (p.34), although rejected by its original buyer, was soon purchased by the Duke of Mantua, on the advice of Rubens, and later passed into the hands of that most discerning connoisseur, King Charles I of England.

Moreover, Caravaggio's earthy style was entirely in tune with the times. His Entombment of Christ (p.32) was commissioned by St Filippo Neri's Oratorian Order, a newly founded populist movement whose advocacy of a simple faith, with a minimum of ritual, and whose insistence that the Apostles were to be thought of as ordinary, everyday people conformed remarkably to the spirit of the painter's work.

In artistic terms, Caravaggio's most telling innovation was his dramatic use of chiaroscuro (see p.20), through which his figures emerged from the shadows into a harsh, spotlit glare, rather like actors on a stage. This feature was rapidly taken up by his many followers throughout Europe, earning them their nickname of the 'Tenebrists' (tenebrae is Latin for darkness).

Sympathy and Insight

The remarkable spread of Caravaggio's ideas emphasizes the internationalism of the Baroque movement. In an age where the major commissions lay in the hands of Church and State, there was a much greater artistic interchange than in, say, the 19th century, when many painters worked independently. Outside Italy, Caravaggio's influence was particularly strong in Spain, France and Holland. The connection with Spain was channelled through Naples, which was then ruled *by Spanish Viceroys. Ribera – the closest of Caravaggio's Spanish disciples – worked in the city after 1616 and Velázquez visited it during his Italian tour of 1629-31.*

However, the legacy of Caravaggio's realism had already been evident in Velázquez's earlier pictures. His bodegones *(examples on pp.50 and 57) demonstrated the same cool detachment as the former's still-life work and even closer was the painting of* Bacchus and his Companions, *where the Caravaggesque figure of the god of wine was surrounded by a group of drinkers who appeared every bit as coarse as the Italian's depictions of the Apostles.*

It is tempting to speculate how Velázquez's

25" × 19½"/Manchester, New Hampshire, The Currier Gallery of Art

Blasted Elm with a View of Edmond aan Zee
(left) In this unusual scene Ruisdael created a complex illusion of space.

The artists
(top to bottom) 19th-century impression of Ruisdael; a self-portrait of Van Dyck; probable self-portrait of Caravaggio; Velazquez in a portrait by an unknown pupil.

style might have developed had he not become attached to the court of Philip IV of Spain. In the event, his naturalism had to be translated into a more regal vein, although his approach remained disconcertingly forthright. Velázquez's portraits of his slave (p.64) and of the King's dwarves (pp.60-61) showed no less sympathy and insight than those which so pitilessly described the unattractive features of his royal master (p.51).

In common with Van Dyck, Velázquez may have found his royal patronage a mixed blessing. On the credit side, it did grant him financial security and considerable status, but it also left him a little time to extend his work beyond portraiture. Paintings like The Surrender of Breda *(pp.58-9) and* The Rokeby Venus *(pp.62-3) offer tantalizing glimpses of other avenues that might have been explored. Ironically, too, Velázquez's duties at Madrid left him rather isolated, since the principal artistic centre was at Seville and, for this reason, his immediate influence was overshadowed by that of Murillo.*

The King's Painter

In England, Van Dyck's dilemma was even greater, since the embargo on holy images in Protestant churches precluded the possibility of any commissions for religious paintings – a field in which he had demonstrated a marked talent early in his career. However, the autocratic monarchies of northern Europe did appreciate the propaganda-value of the grand Baroque style and were keen to harness it for the glorification of their own regimes. The most sought-after painter in this respect was Peter Paul Rubens, whose Marie de' Medici cycle in Paris and whose ceiling for Charles I's Banqueting House in London are acknowledged masterpieces of Baroque decorative art.

As a young man, Van Dyck worked as Rubens' assistant in his native Antwerp, and his ambition must have been fired by the power and scope of the older man's achievements. Consequently, many of his early works bore the stamp of Rubens' style and it was only after his trip to Italy that Van Dyck's individuality blossomed.

The greatest single influence was Titian. Van Dyck is reported to have owned as many as nineteen works by the Venetian master and, doubtless, he would have had access to more through the collections of the Duke of Arundel and Charles I. From Titian, he adopted a looser, more informal approach to composition and a rich, painterly technique. These qualities enabled Van Dyck to revolutionize artistic standards in England, producing not only an undying image of Charles I's doomed Court, but also helping him to create an immense range of designs that generations of native portraitists were to follow.

The Lyrical Master

Outside portraiture, England's receptiveness to Baroque tendencies was severely limited. In Holland, however, the impact of the movement was even more modest (with the sole exception of Utrecht, which was a Catholic centre). Holland was democratic, Protestant and bourgeois, and these factors generated an entirely different atmosphere and art market.

The keynote of the Baroque was grandeur – either in scale or in tone – and this proved alien to the new Dutch Republic. There, private collectors preferred small, cabinet paintings which reflected everyday life. As a result, local artists specialized in landscape, genre or still-life subjects, rather than in the more exalted themes of religious or history painting. Ruisdael, significantly, was the only artist in this volume who did not feel the need to journey to Italy. Indeed, the closest contact he made with Italianate sources was during his trip to Germany, when he saw works by the much-travelled landscapist, Adam Elsheimer.

Indirectly, however, his style did betray some influences from the artistic currents prevailing in Europe. Ruisdael worked on a larger scale than most of his fellow-countrymen and the frequently sombre tone of his pictures marked a deliberate break from the more decorative tradition of artists like Jan van Goyen. He also employed brilliant lighting contrasts to instil a dramatic sense of realism into his landscapes.

Nonetheless, the pervasive air of foreboding in his work – typified by looming stormclouds, gusty seas and (one of his favourite devices) the introduction of felled or withering trees into a fertile landscape (for example, p.112) – brought Ruisdael closer to the spirit of the Romantics. The Romantic movement was, in fact, the eventual heir to the emotional side of the Baroque, with its extremes of passions and its taste for violence, while the technical aspects of the style – its florid execution and its dynamism – gradually merged into the virtuosity of Rococo art.

Giraudon

Caravaggio/Detail: David with the Head of Goliath/Borghese Gallery, Rome

CARAVAGGIO

1571-1610

Caravaggio was one of the most extraordinary characters in the history of art. He was not only the most powerful and influential Italian painter of the 17th century, but also one of the prototypes of the idea of the artist as a rebel outside the normal conventions of society. His tempestuous career was punctuated by disputes with patrons about his unconventional treatment of religious themes and by a series of acts of physical violence.

After a struggle to establish himself in Rome, Caravaggio had achieved widespread fame by his early 30s, his dramatic use of light and shade and uncompromising realism creating a new pictorial vocabulary for European art. At the height of his career, however, he fled Rome after killing a man, and the rest of his short life was spent restlessly moving from place to place. Caravaggio died aged 38.

Violent by Nature

Caravaggio's fiery temper and unruly behaviour led to numerous encounters with the police and the grisly crime of murder. The last years of his tragic life were spent as a fugitive from justice.

Michelangelo Merisi, the son of Fermo di Bernardino Merisi, was born in 1571, probably in Milan, not far from the village of Caravaggio where his family came from (and which he named himself after some 20 years later). His father, who was *majordomo* (head butler) to Francesco Sforza, Marchese di Caravaggio, died in 1577, and Michelangelo, with two brothers (one of whom died in 1588) and a sister, was brought up by his mother, Lucia Aratori.

In 1584, at the age of 12, Michelangelo joined the workshop of the Milanese painter Simone Peterzano as an apprentice. Nothing else is known about his early life, except that his mother died in 1590, and two years later Michelangelo, his brother and his sister divided the family property between them. Michelangelo inherited 393 imperial pounds, which enabled him to set off for Rome where successive popes had embarked on ambitious schemes to embellish the town, and the prospect of large and lucrative commissions attracted painters, sculptors and architects from all over Italy and beyond.

With large numbers of Italian and foreign painters flooding the Roman market, the going was bound to be tough for a young, inexperienced artist trained by a minor provincial master. Caravaggio should have been able to live comfortably for several years on his inheritance

Lombardy upbringing
(right) Michelangelo Merisi grew up in the family home in Caravaggio, a village surrounded by Lombardy countryside.

M. Pedone/The Image Bank

A Milanese training
(below) After a four-year apprenticeship in Milan, Caravaggio left for Rome. He was rumoured to have fled because of a murder, but it is more likely that he was attracted by better prospects in Rome.

Jean-Loup Charmet

Painting in Rome
(below right) Soon after his arrival in Rome, Caravaggio was taken into the household of Cavaliere d'Arpino, and probably helped the painter with his numerous fresco commissions for churches in the city.

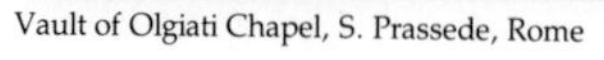

Vault of Olgiati Chapel, S. Prassede, Rome

Sick Bacchus
(right) This early work is one of a series of sensual self-portraits which Caravaggio painted after leaving Cavaliere d'Arpino's employment. The artist's sickly complexion may reflect his recent hospitalization.

Mauro Pucciarelli

Borghese Gallery, Rome

Key Dates

1571 born in Lombardy, possibly in Milan

c.1592 moves to Rome

c.1595 enters the household of Cardinal Del Monte

1599 gains first major public commission – paintings for the Contarelli chapel in San Luigi dei Francesi

1600 paints works for the Cerasi Chapel in Sta Maria del Popolo; name begins to appear in police records

1605 wounds a notary defending his prostitute mistress

1606 kills a tennis opponent and flees to Naples

1607 travels to Malta

1608 made a Knight; travels to Sicily

1609 returns to Naples and is badly wounded

1610 dies of a fever at Port'Ercole

but true to his later lifestyle, he seems to have spent it quickly and unwisely and his early years in Rome were marked by poverty.

There are no documents which record Caravaggio's activities in the Holy City until 1599. It is generally agreed, however, that at some point he was employed by Giuseppe Cesari, the Cavaliere d'Arpino, one of the leading fresco-painters of the day, who was working on huge papal and ecclesiastical commissions. Yet even this promising association came to an abrupt end when Caravaggio was committed to hospital, the *Ospedale della Consolazione* – according to one source, because he had been kicked by a horse.

AN INFLUENTIAL PATRON

Some time later, Caravaggio attracted the attention of Cardinal Del Monte, a wealthy and sophisticated cleric, collector of paintings, lover of music, and official cardinal-protector of the *Accademia di San Luca*, the painters' academy in Rome. Del Monte represented the interests of Florence at the papal court and resided in the Medici Palazzo Madama, near the Piazza Navona.

Caravaggio became a member of the Cardinal's household, was given lodgings, food and a regular allowance, and he painted, in response, a number of pictures of rather effeminate young men. That Del Monte was a discreet hedonist, dallying with young boys, and that Caravaggio shared this taste, has often been inferred from these early works; and even in later, publicly displayed altarpieces, we find Caravaggio including angels of an alluringly androgynous nature. On the other hand, some of the most overtly erotic depictions of young boys, including the *Victorious Cupid* (p.19), were painted for patrons who were beyond any suspicion of homoerotic inclinations. And it is surprising that at a time when homosexuality was considered a serious crime, no suspicion seems to have fallen on Caravaggio himself. Had there been any doubts about him, the many enemies he managed to make in his short life would have exploited them publicly and with relish. What gave rise to rumours was the dubious reputation of his girlfriend Lena, a prostitute, whom he was said to have used as the model for some of his depictions of the Virgin Mary.

All of Caravaggio's early paintings were relatively small works, still-lifes, genre-scenes and a few occasional religious subjects. They were produced either for particular patrons, like Del Monte or the Prior of the *Ospedale della Consolazione*, or for the open market, to be sold by picture dealers. This was not the way to become rich and famous. In the course of the Counter Reformation, Rome was witnessing an unprecedented building-boom of new churches, and each new church required chapel-decorations and altarpieces. This

A struggling artist
(below) In his early years Caravaggio was forced to work for other artists who sold their works on the open market.

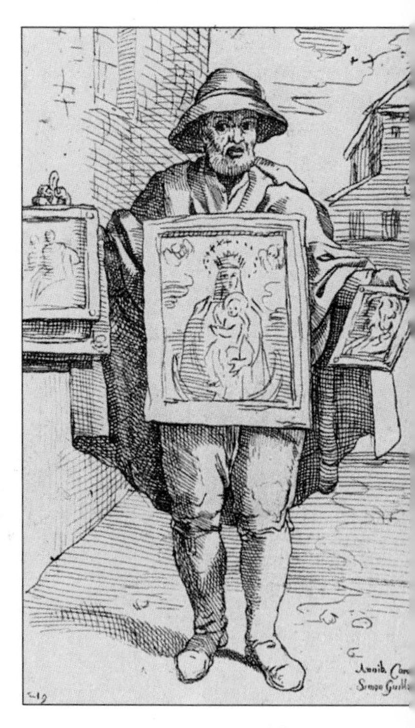

was where the big money was and where public reputations were established. Caravaggio, now in his late 20s, must have been desperate to be given the chance to compete in this lucrative market.

The chance came in 1599 with the commission of two large paintings for the Contarelli Chapel in San Luigi dei Francesi. The church is only a few steps down the street from the Palazzo Madama, and Cardinal Del Monte was probably instrumental in securing this important contract for his *protégé*.

AMBITIOUS PAINTINGS

Never before, as far as we know, had Caravaggio attempted anything on a comparable scale. And x-ray photographs of the *Martyrdom of St Matthew* have revealed his initial uncertainty. He was fumbling about for the right size of his figures and for a convincing composition. After several attempts to improve and correct his original version he was forced to start all over again. Yet the final outcome seems to have been an overwhelming success; even Caravaggio's arch-enemy, the painter Giovanni Baglione, who later wrote a *Life of Caravaggio*, admitted that much: 'This commission made Caravaggio famous', he wrote, and added maliciously, 'and the paintings were excessively praised by evil people.'

This was Caravaggio's breakthrough. Large commissions followed one another in quick succession, and after a couple of years, the painter's fame had spread right across Europe. The Dutch art-historian Karel van Mander, living in Haarlem, wrote in 1603: 'There is a certain Michelangelo da Caravaggio, who is doing extraordinary things in Rome.' Yet it was not only the news of the painter's talent that had reached van Mander; he had also been informed of Caravaggio's notorious life-style and violent behaviour: 'He does not study his art constantly, so that after two weeks of work he will sally forth for two months with his rapier at his side and his servant-boy after him, going from one tennis court to another, always ready to argue or fight, so that he is impossible to get along with.' While van Mander's information about Caravaggio's paintings was inaccurate, that about his public behaviour was correct.

From 1600 onward, since his first great public success, Caravaggio appeared regularly in the protocols of the Roman police: in November of that year he attacked a colleague with a stick, and the following February he was brought before the magistrates, accused of having raised his sword against a soldier. In 1603, Giovanni Baglione brought a libel action against Caravaggio and

The Generous Cardinal

Cardinal Francesco Del Monte was Caravaggio's first great patron. He became a cardinal in 1588 and had considerable influence at the papal court. A rich man, Del Monte fully indulged his great love of painting and music, and was renowned for his hedonistic lifestyle. Before he met Caravaggio – in about 1595 – and took him into his household, the painter was, in Baglione's words, 'in a deplorable condition, without money and practically in rags.' The cardinal was responsible, more than anyone else, for launching Caravaggio on his successful career.

Rogers Fund, 1952

The Metropolitan Museum of Art, New York

Mauro Pucciarelli

Decorations for the Contarelli Chapel
(left) In 1599 Caravaggio received his first major commission for the two paintings of the life of St Matthew which decorate the side walls of the Contarelli Chapel. The altarpiece was added in 1603.

G. Annunziata/Explorer

Gregory Heisler/The Image Bank

The Musicians
(left) Caravaggio's first work for his patron was designed to appeal to the cardinal's liking for young boys. The lute-player may be the artist's close friend, Mario Minnitti.

Luxurious lodgings
(above) The cardinal's home was the splendid Palazzo Madama. Caravaggio was given a room in the vast Medici palace, together with an allowance, and bread and wine.

Criminal exploits
(above and left) From 1600 on, Caravaggio became notorious for his brawls. He would roam the streets at night, with his servant and dog, ready for a fight. In May 1605 he was jailed for carrying arms: a scribe at the trial sketched his sword and dagger.

Model and mistress
(below) In two of his paintings Caravaggio is thought to have modelled the Virgin on Lena, his girlfriend and a prostitute. In 1605, Caravaggio attacked a notary for pestering her, and in the ensuing complaint she was described as 'Lena who stands in the Piazza Navona'.

others; the painter was briefly imprisoned and released only on condition that he stayed at home and promised not to offend Baglione – any breach of these conditions would lead to him being made a galley slave. In April 1604, he was accused of having thrown a dish of hot artichokes in the face of a waiter in a restaurant, and of having threatened him with his sword. Later in the same year he was arrested for insulting a policeman. In 1605 he was arrested for carrying a sword and a dagger without permission; brought before the magistrates for insulting a lady and her daughter, and for attacking a notary in a quarrel over his girlfriend; and finally he was accused by his landlady of not paying his rent and of throwing stones through her windows.

Perhaps we should judge Caravaggio's character not simply by his criminal records and his violent behaviour. He was supported and protected by some of the most sophisticated patrons in Rome, including Del Monte and the Marchese Giustiniani. Some of his best friends and companions in his rakish adventures were well-educated and refined men. Giovanni Battista Marino, perhaps the most erudite and cultivated poet of the age, had his portrait painted by Caravaggio and immortalized his art in his poems. And while Caravaggio's public statements about

Caravaggio/Detail: Madonna dei Palafrenieri/Borghese Gallery, Rome/Scala

earlier and contemporary artists could appear brutish and simplistic, he privately studied the art of Leonardo, Raphael, Michelangelo, and the great Venetian painters with considerable sensitivity and a fine understanding. We simply do not know enough about his intimate life, his interests or learning to form a fuller and more just image of his character than that provided by the criminal records of the Roman police.

On 28 May 1606, Caravaggio's violent temper finally led to disaster: unwilling to pay a wager of 10 scudi on a tennis match, he and several friends got involved in a fierce fight with his opponent, a certain Ranuccio Tommasoni, and his friends on the Campo Marzo. The painter was badly wounded, and so was one of his supporters, a Captain Petronio, who was subsequently imprisoned. Tommasoni, however, died from Caravaggio's attack.

A fatal tennis match
(below) Caravaggio's violent activities culminated in murder. On 28 May 1606 he and some friends were involved in a brawl over a wager on a tennis match. Caravaggio was badly wounded, but his opponent was killed. The artist went into hiding and then fled Rome.

The Mansell Collection

J. Allan Cash

FLIGHT FROM ROME

The painter went into hiding for three days, probably in the palace of the Marchese Giustiniani, and then fled secretly from Rome, which he was never to see again. Caravaggio's exact whereabouts over the next five months are unclear. By October 1606 he was in Naples, well outside papal jurisdiction. In less than a year he completed at least three major altarpieces, waiting impatiently for his influential friends and patrons in Rome to secure a papal pardon which would allow him to return. Yet the authorities were slow to respond, and in July 1607 Caravaggio left Naples and arrived on the island of Malta.

Whether he undertook the trip to Malta of his own accord, presumably in the hope of being made a Knight of St John, or whether he had been invited by the Maltese Knights to paint certain pictures, we do not know. But Caravaggio's stay on the island was productive: in addition to portraits, among them that of the Grandmaster Alof de Wignacourt (opposite), he painted his largest work ever, the *Beheading of St John* (pp.18-19), the patron-saint of the Knights' Order.

On 14 July 1608, Caravaggio was made a Knight of the Order of Obedience, obviously as a reward for his work. In addition, Bellori reports, 'the Grandmaster put a gold chain around his neck and made him a gift of two Turkish slaves, along with other signs of esteem and appreciation for his work.' Caravaggio was not to enjoy the benefits of his new honour for very long. According to Bellori, his 'tormented nature' led him into an ill-considered quarrel with a noble knight. Perhaps

The Knights of Malta

Caravaggio arrived in Malta in July 1607 in the hope of becoming a Knight of St John. The Knights Hospitaler of St John are the oldest surviving order of chivalry, founded to protect pilgrims in Jerusalem. They were driven out of the Holy Land in 1291 and were virtually homeless until 1530, when Charles V conferred on them sovereignty of Malta. Caravaggio was received into the Order on 14 July 1608, but his violent ways caught up with him and he was expelled only five months later 'like a foul and putrid limb'.

Maltese paintings
(right and below) Caravaggio was made an honorary Knight in thanks for his portraits of Alof de Wignacourt. The Beheading of St John the Baptist, *painted for the Cathedral of Valetta, includes the artist's only signature, written in blood – a reflection of Caravaggio's disturbed mental state.*

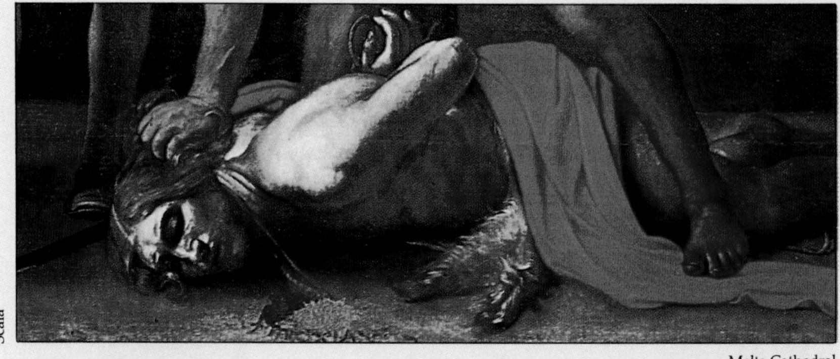

Scala

Malta Cathedral

A fugitive in Naples
(left) Caravaggio probably arrived on the streets of Naples in the autumn following the murder of his tennis opponent. While there, the artist painted a series of ecclesiastical works while he waited for the papal pardon which would allow him to return to Rome.

the news of his Roman crime had caught up with him: in any case, Caravaggio was thrown into prison. He managed to escape by night and fled to Sicily. The Knights of Malta subsequently stripped the artist of all his honours and excluded him from the Order.

After short stays in Syracuse, Messina and Palermo, and the rapid completion of major altarpieces in each of these towns, Caravaggio returned to Naples. His fame enabled him to request and receive large payments for each work he undertook, but he was still a fugitive, by now perhaps not only from papal justice but also that of the Maltese Knights. By October 1609 rumours had reached Rome that he had been killed or badly wounded in Naples. According to Baglione, 'his enemy finally caught up with him and he was so severely slashed in the face that he was almost unrecognizable.'

In Rome, Caravaggio's friends were still pressing for a pardon, now supported by Cardinal Ferdinando Gonzaga, who had bought his *Death of the Virgin* (p.34) after it had been rejected by the priests of Sta Maria della Scala. In the summer of 1610, Caravaggio left Naples suddenly and set sail, on a small boat, to Port'Ercole, a port about 80 miles north of Rome which was under Spanish protection. It is clear that he was expecting to be able to return to Rome very soon but could not yet enter papal territory. After four unhappy years of restlessness he could look forward with confidence to rejoining his friends and patrons in the Holy City. But this was not to happen.

Baglione, Caravaggio's old enemy, has left us the most vivid account of the artist's last days. Having gone ashore in Port'Ercole, Caravaggio 'was mistakenly captured and held for two days in prison and when he was released, his boat was no longer to be found. This made him furious, and in desperation he started out along the beach under the fierce heat of the summer sun, trying to catch sight of the vessel that had his belongings. Finally, he came to a place where he was put to bed with a raging fever; and so, without the aid of God or man, in a few days he died, as miserably as he had lived.' Caravaggio died on 18 July 1610; he was not even 40 years old.

An untimely end
(below) Caravaggio died of a malignant fever on 18 July 1610 at Port' Ercole – a Spanish garrison town which bordered on the Papal States. Anticipating a pardon from Pope Paul V, Caravaggio had been making his way back to the Holy City when he was mistakenly imprisoned. On his release he found his boat had disappeared and wandered along the sun-scorched beaches until he collapsed from a fever. The pardon he had been awaiting for four years was finally granted, but too late for Caravaggio.

Réunion des Muséss Nationaux

Alof de Wignacourt/Louvre, Paris

Giancarlo Costa

Fierce Originality

Caravaggio's dramatic and often violent compositions are the result of his stubborn disregard for convention, his passionate belief in the individual and his uncompromising realism.

We know of other artists with violent temperaments, unruly lifestyles and criminal records, but in the work of no other painter is a sense of brutal violence so openly displayed as in that of Caravaggio. Whether we are looking at the *Sacrifice of Abraham* (p.26), the *Judith Beheading Holofernes* (p.27), or the *Beheading of St John* (below right), we are struck by the deliberate brutality and aggression of the depiction. We see swords cutting through throats, blood not just flowing but streaming, or the finger of St Thomas physically probing the wound in Christ's side. That a civilized man like John Ruskin saw in Caravaggio's art 'definite signs of an evil mind, ill repressed . . . the perpetual seeking for and feeding upon horror and ugliness, and filthiness of sin', is not altogether surprising, given the totally different times in which the two men lived.

Within the context of the Italian Counter-Reformation, however, there were traditions of thinking about art to which Caravaggio's paintings relate naturally and easily. The sacred events of the

Scala

Ambrosiana, Milan

Still-Life (c.1598)
(above) Caravaggio was originally trained as a still-life painter, but only one of his still-life compositions has survived. The illusionistic approach and unstinting naturalism give it a tremendous physical power.

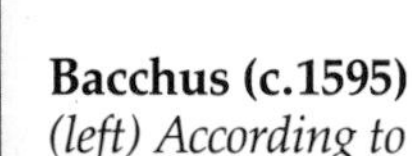

Scala

Uffizi, Florence

Bacchus (c.1595)
(left) According to an early biographer, the artist painted this portrait from his own image in a mirror. The androgynous Bacchus is shown in a provocative pose, displaying his rounded, plump shoulder and lazily fingering his velvet bow. The overripe still-life and the god's dirty fingernails are striking examples of Caravaggio's realism.

Scala

Scala

Uffizi, Florence

Bildarchiv Preussischer Multurbesitz

Staatliche Museen, Berlin

Malta Cathedral

Medusa (c.1597)
(above) Caravaggio's painted shield with the severed head of Medusa is one of his most horrifying images and a precocious display of virtuosity.

Victorious Cupid (1601/2)
(above right) This blatantly erotic work was painted for Marchese Giustiniani, who prized it above all the other pictures in his collection. The thinly disguised subject matter and little details like the feather which gently brushes against the boy's thigh, still give the painting its extraordinary ability to shock.

The Beheading of St John the Baptist (1608)
(left) This late masterpiece, painted two years before Caravaggio's death, is remarkable for its daring use of empty space. The composition is carefully balanced and the sombre colour-scheme is dramatically enlivened by the flame red of St John's robe.

Gospels should be presented in such a way that the public could identify with them, could see them almost as happening in front of their eyes. The dirty feet and wrinkled faces of Caravaggio's peasant-like figures, or the swollen corpse of the dead Virgin are not signs of social rebellion; they are attempts to render the stories of the New Testament as realistically as possible, as involving real people – not the stale, dignified figures of saints, raised to an elevated and bloodless state well above that of the normal human condition by centuries of official Church art.

TRUE TO NATURE

This is at the heart of Caravaggio's naturalism, as reported as early as 1603 by Van Mander: 'His belief is that all art is nothing but a bagatelle or children's work . . . unless it is done after life, and that we can do no better than to follow nature.' Caravaggio was even impatient with the conditions of pictorial depiction: the elbow of the disciple in the London *Supper at Emmaus* (pp.28-9) seems to poke through the picture's surface, and the first version of the altarpiece of *St Matthew* for the Contarelli Chapel was rejected by the clergy because the Saint's dirty foot was sticking out of the picture exactly at the eye-level of a priest saying Mass in front of it. The figures in the *Entombment of Christ* (p.32) for the Chiesa Nuova seem to be lowering the dead body of the Saviour out of the picture and onto the real altar below.

Caravaggio's famous *chiaroscuro* – his habit of clothing his scenes in darkness with the main figures picked out by strong beams of concentrated light – should also be seen in this context. Some later critics saw it as an admission that he could not paint detailed backgrounds; others assumed that he always worked in a dark cellar lit by only one small window. It is probably true that he had only a limited mastery of perspective and was unable to arrange his figures in complex spatial settings; in almost all his pictures, the figures are placed in a shallow foreground-space against a background of impenetrable blackness. The modern tourist can see those of his works which have remained in their original setting in churches and chapels by slotting 200-lira pieces into a little machine which will then illuminate the paintings, for a couple of minutes, with strong beams of electric light. This totally destroys the intended effect. In Caravaggio's day, the main source of illumination was oil-lamps and dozens or hundreds of small candles ranged in front of altarpieces. In their dim light, the figures of Caravaggio's pictures would have stood out not only against their own dark background, but also against that of the surrounding space: they would have appeared to the beholder with an uncanny sense of presence and reality.

Yet the light in Caravaggio's art is more than a mere means of illumination, of showing figures to the spectator. It is an active force in his

The Calling of St Matthew (1599-1600)
(right and detail below) Caravaggio's version of this story, which is only briefly mentioned in the Bible, shows the tax collector Matthew in the company of his friends. They are seated round a table counting their takings – very much in the manner of Caravaggio's early Cardsharper paintings. The dramatic beam of light which illuminates the shrouded figure of Christ and follows his outstretched arm, leads us to the figure of Matthew who is identified by his incredulous gesture. Caravaggio has given the theme a new relevance and modernity by using flamboyant contemporary costumes and lively poses for Matthew's companions.

Scala

TRADEMARKS

Chiaroscuro

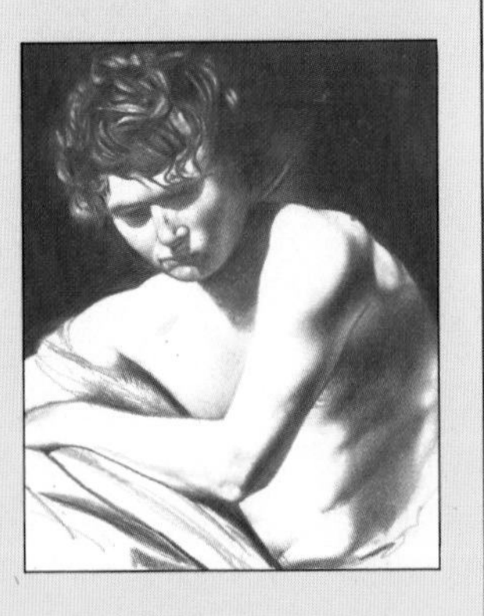

Caravaggio's exaggerated use of *chiaroscuro* – light-dark – is very striking. His figures are lit by a strong, raking light which casts deep, black shadows. They emerge from their gloomy surroundings in dramatic relief.

S. Luigi dei Francesi, Rome

composition and, in many cases, it is not a realistic light at all. The full power of Christ's *Calling of St Matthew* (left) is made visibly manifest by the sharp and cutting edge of the light which accompanies his beckoning gesture. And St Paul, in the picture of his conversion, seems to have been thrown to the ground and transfixed by the dazzling light from above (p.30).

PROVOCATIVE IMAGES

Many critics, from the 17th and 19th century, accused Caravaggio of having been unable to draw. They claimed he could only paint with the live model in front of his eyes, copying it as accurately as possible: being servile to nature, he could not attain the heights of idealistic art, as Annibale Carracci and his successors had done. Caravaggio's own statements had, of course, provoked these criticisms, and there were rumours that for the *Death of the Virgin* (p.34) he had used the swollen corpse of a prostitute as a model, or that, in painting the *Raising of Lazarus*, he had forced his horrified models to hold up a decaying corpse by threatening to attack them with his dagger.

In the terms of 'high art', epitomized by the sculptures of ancient Greece and Rome, and by the High Renaissance masterpieces of Raphael and Michelangelo, Caravaggio's realism appeared as vulgar, rude and provocative, lacking in *decorum*, grace and beauty. And it was not only aesthetically-minded critics who objected to his brutal and down-to-earth style, but also clergymen: more than one of his religious commissions, to the painter's despair, were rejected by priests (only to be quickly acquired by more discerning private collectors).

It is true that no drawing has survived that could be attributed, with any degree of certainty, to Caravaggio. The effects he was aiming at, the dramatic light and the sense of reality and presence of his figures, could not have been anticipated and planned in small-scale drawings. Like the great Venetian masters of the 16th century, Giorgione and Titian in particular, he seems to have painted straight onto the canvas, working out his compositions as he went along. In many cases this necessitated changes, adjustments and repainting. Yet Caravaggio was a fast painter who, unlike many of his better-behaved colleagues, normally delivered his work on time. This was certainly less the result of an unexpected conscientiousness, and more a sign of his quick and impatient temper. There is no indication that he ever painted in fresco, the technique regarded as most prestigious and most suitable for large-scale decorations. Fresco-painting required careful planning and a slow and patient execution – procedures which were not congenial to Caravaggio's approach to art. And the restrained colours of this medium would not have enabled him to place before the eyes of his spectators, and in dramatic relief, religious figures who looked like them, dressed like them, and seemed to behave like them.

COMPARISONS

Fruit and Flowers

The still-life genre did not become established in European painting until the 17th century, and Caravaggio was one of the key figures in its development. He not only painted superb still-life details, but was also among the first to paint still-lifes for their own sake, declaring that 'it took as much skill to paint a good picture of flowers as of figures'.

Lauros Giraudon

Museo Nazionale, Naples

Wadsworth Atheneum, Hartford, Connecticut

Roman Still-Life
(left) Still-life was well known in the classical world and one of the most famous anecdotes told about an ancient artist relates how the painter Zeuxis depicted grapes with such skill that birds flew at the canvas to peck at them, thinking they were real.

Follower of Caravaggio Fruit and Flowers
(above) This still-life was once thought to be by Caravaggio, although it is now considered to be the work of a follower. Such paintings concentrate as much on the symbolism of fruit and flowers as on virtuoso display.

THE MAKING OF A MASTERPIECE

Supper at Emmaus

The *Supper at Emmaus* is one of Caravaggio's finest works, and there is no better example of his ability to jolt the spectator with his uncanny ability to create a sense of actuality. Striking, rhetorical gestures command our attention, elbows and hands seem to project beyond the picture plane and the marvellously painted still-life details look almost tangible. The picture is not well documented; it is not known for whom it was painted and scholars disagree over its dating, although most now put it within a year or two of 1600. The subject concerns one of Christ's appearances to His disciples after His Resurrection. The Bible names only one of the disciples – Cleophas (presumably on the left here); the other wears a scallop shell, the attribute of St James the Greater, but here alluding to pilgrims in general (the disciples were journeying to Emmaus near Jerusalem when they met Jesus, whom they did not immediately recognize). The sharply observed standing figure is the innkeeper.

'Then their eyes were opened, and they recognized Him.'

Luke 24:31

Seeing the light
(left) Caravaggio has chosen to show the disciples at the moment of recognition. Cleophas pushes back his chair in astonishment, almost propelling it out of the picture with the suddenness of his movement.

The evening meal
(below) The spread on the table includes bread and wine, symbols of the Eucharist, a roasted fowl and a basket of decaying fruit – possibly an allusion to man's mortality and the vanity of earthly things.

The National Gallery, London

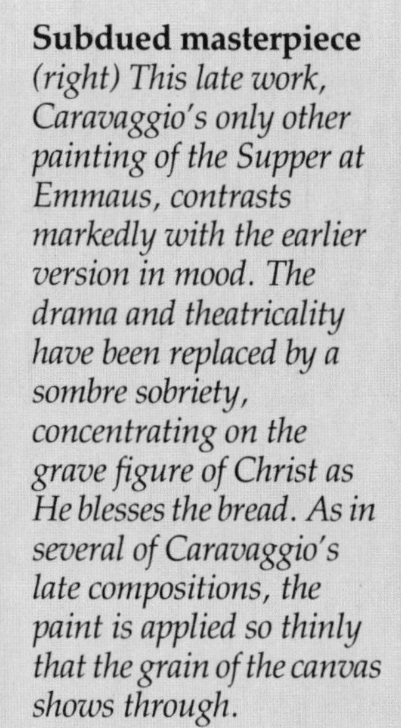

Subdued masterpiece
(right) This late work, Caravaggio's only other painting of the Supper at Emmaus, contrasts markedly with the earlier version in mood. The drama and theatricality have been replaced by a sombre sobriety, concentrating on the grave figure of Christ as He blesses the bread. As in several of Caravaggio's late compositions, the paint is applied so thinly that the grain of the canvas shows through.

Scala

Brera, Milan

True theatre
(right) The second disciple flings out his arms in a gesture of utter amazement, so that his left hand almost 'punctures' the picture surface. In the interests of dramatic effect – and contrary to the laws governing perspective – Caravaggio has shown the disciple's right hand just as large as his left hand even though they are held apart.

Symbolic fruits
(below) Grapes, figs and pomegranates are often represented in art as symbols of Christ's Passion. The grapes, for example, symbolize the Eucharistic wine and therefore the blood of Christ. The pomegranate, because of its mythical associations, symbolizes the Resurrection.

Passion Fruit

Gallery

Caravaggio's early work includes some splendidly flamboyant genre scenes such as The Gipsy Fortune Teller, but he soon found that his true vocation was religious painting and after he began achieving public success when he was in his late 20s, he rarely painted anything other than serious religious works. Often, however, he ran into trouble with his

Réunion des Musées Nationaux

The Gipsy Fortune Teller *c.1594-5*
39″ × 54″ Louvre, Paris

Caravaggio's biographer Bellori tells us how he 'called a gipsy who chanced to pass in the street, and having led her to his inn, portrayed her in the act of predicting the future, as these women of the Egyptian race are wont to do'. The foppish man, who is evidently smitten with the girl, does not notice she is removing his ring.

patrons, who found his revolutionary realism too strong for their tastes. Both the Madonna di Loreto and The Death of the Virgin caused scandals because he was felt to have represented religious scenes without due respect. His down-to-earth approach, however, became hugely influential, as did his powerful handling of light and shade, seen at its most striking in The Conversion of St Paul and The Crucifixion of St Peter.

Caravaggio's approach became more introspective as he matured. The Early Supper at Emmaus, for example, is a brilliant showpiece, but the late David with the Head of Goliath has an air of solemn, brooding tragedy.

Scala

The Rest on the Flight into Egypt *c.1594-5*
41¾" × 33¼" Doria-Pamphili Gallery, Rome

Caravaggio's mature paintings are usually very strong, bold images, but here his youthful ardour (and inexperience) shows in the multiplicity of beautiful details, which do not quite blend into an entirely convincing whole. The seductive, almost nude angel, whose beauty seems anything but celestial, was particularly praised by Bellori.

Giraudon

The Sacrifice of Abraham *c.1603-04*
41″ × 35″ Uffizi, Florence

This painting is unusual in Caravaggio's work in that it includes a relatively detailed landscape background. The subject is treated with remarkable savagery, stressing the brutality of a human sacrifice – Abraham's face is unnecessarily severe as he forces down the head of his screaming son.

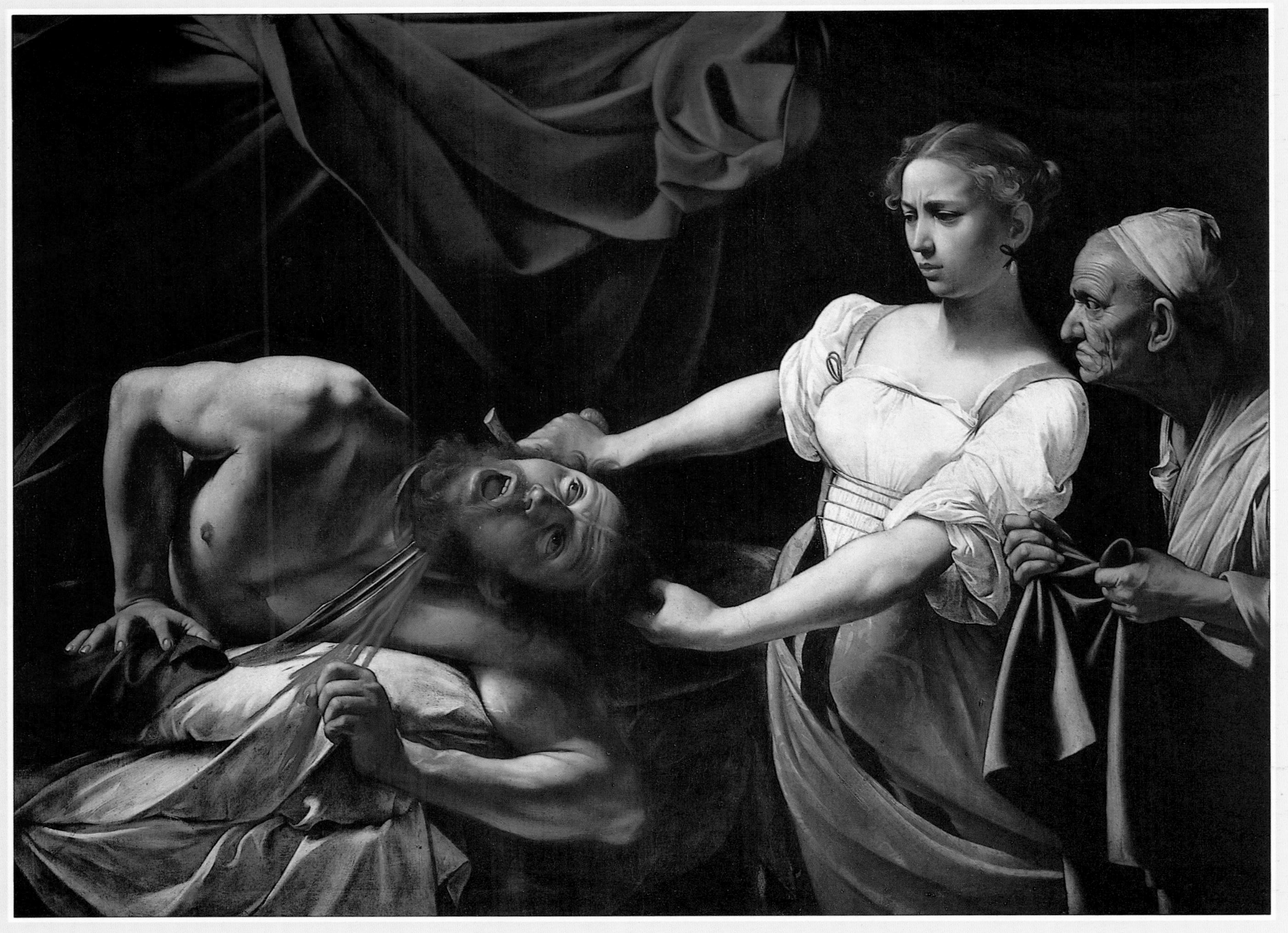

Scala

Judith Beheading Holofernes *c.1598-9*
56½" × 76¾" Palazzo Barberini, Rome

In earlier depictions of the subject, the Jewish heroine Judith is usually shown holding the severed head of the enemy general she has killed, but Caravaggio gives us the full, undiluted horror of the death agony; she appears almost to be sawing his head off.

The Supper at Emmaus *c.1600-01*
55½" × 77¼" National Gallery, London

Caravaggio is usually characterized as a rebel against tradition, but he learnt much from the art of the past, particularly his North Italian heritage. The composition of this painting, for example, owes a good deal to Titian's well-known representation of the subject (now in the Louvre), and the bold gestures recall the words of Leonardo that the painter has to use actions to represent 'the passions of the soul'. (Caravaggio was trained in Milan, where Leonardo spent the greater part of his career and could well have been familiar with his ideas.) The brilliant foreshortening brings to mind another great Renaissance artist, Mantegna. Caravaggio, however, makes of the subject something completely personal, and although the painting is not documented, it is of such quality and so distinctively in his powerful style that its attribution has never been questioned. The moment represented comes from Luke 24: 30-31. The two disciples of Christ had not recognized Him when, after the Resurrection, He had fallen in with them on the road to Emmaus. But when He was at the table with them, at the moment He blessed and broke the bread, the scales fell from their eyes.

Scala

The Conversion of St Paul *1600-01*
90½″ × 68¾″ Cerasi Chapel, Santa Maria del Popolo, Rome

This picture forms a pair with the St Peter opposite, and the two works are still in the chapel for which they were painted. The disturbing foreshortening and dramatic perspective, based on a strong diagonal movement, are due to the fact that the paintings were designed to be looked at side on.

Scala

The Crucifixion of St Peter *1600-01*
90½" × 68¾" Cerasi Chapel, Santa Maria del Popolo, Rome

St Peter chose to be crucified upside down, and Caravaggio has represented the scene with astonishing immediacy. As the workers struggle and strain to raise the cross in the darkness, St Peter slowly lifts his head in a final act of rebellion, his eyes glazed with pain and physical exertion.

Mauro Pucciarelli

The Entombment of Christ *1602-04*
118″ × 80″ Vatican Picture Gallery, Rome

Until the 19th century, this was undoubtedly Caravaggio's most acclaimed painting – probably because it is the most traditional and uncontroversial of his major works. With the exception of the chunky, heavily veined legs of the figure on the right, the forms are idealized by Caravaggio's standards. Rubens and Fragonard copied the painting.

Mauro Pucciarelli

The Madonna di Loreto *c.1603-05*
102″ × 59″ Sant'Agostino, Rome

This altarpiece brings to life a famous statuary group at Loreto, which was said to have the miraculous power 'to succour the unfortunate and the meek' and to intercede for pilgrims. The populace, according to Caravaggio's enemy, Baglione, were shocked by the man's 'muddy feet' and the woman's 'messy and dirty bonnet'.

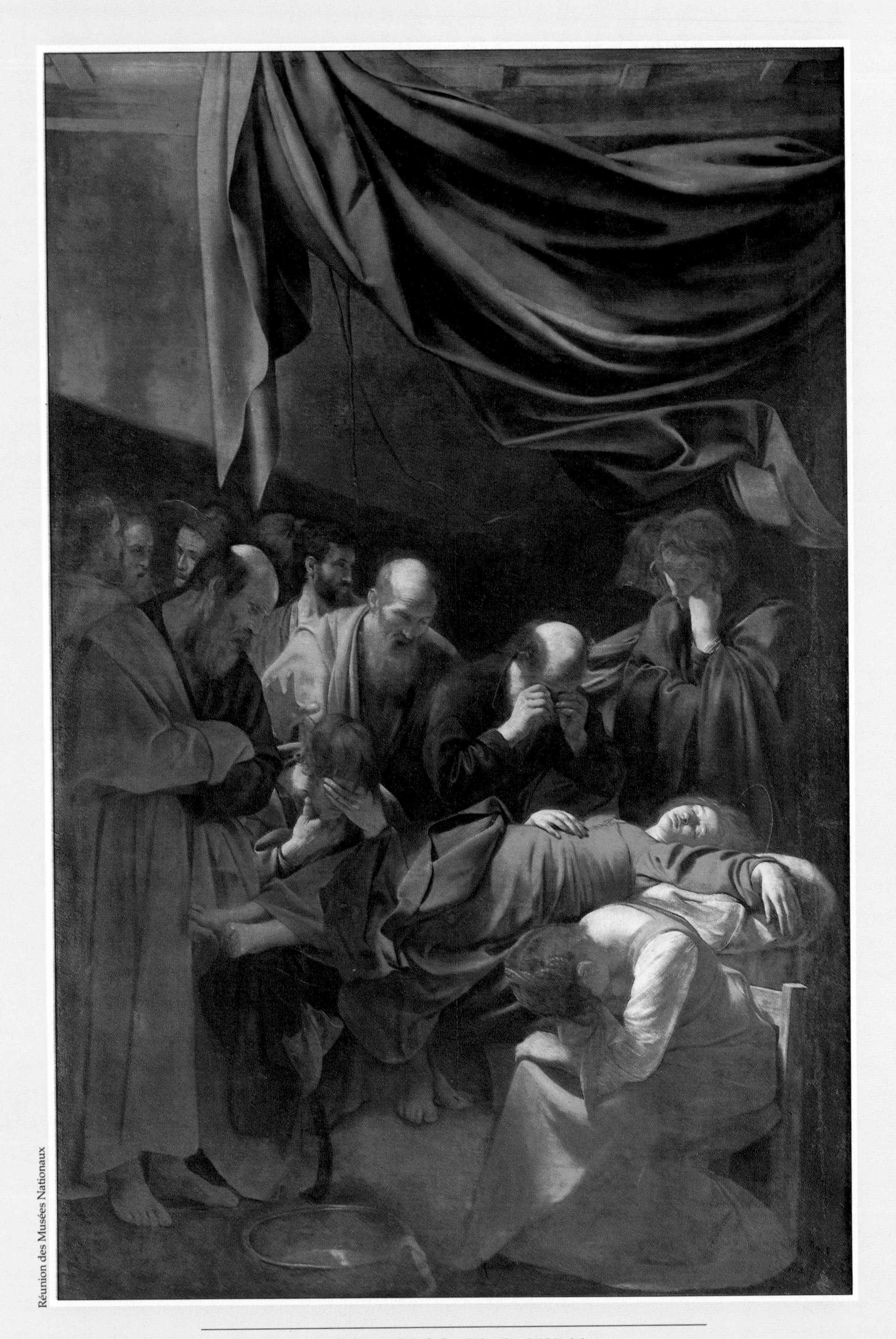

Réunion des Musées Nationaux

The Death of the Virgin *1605-06*
145¼″ × 96½″ Louvre, Paris

Caravaggio painted this huge altarpiece for the church of Santa Maria della Scala. Despite its grandeur and incredible poignancy, the work was rejected on the grounds of decorum, as it showed 'the Madonna bloated and with her legs uncovered' (Baglione) and because rumour had it that Caravaggio's model was 'a dirty whore from the Ortaccio'.

Giraudon

David with the Head of Goliath *c.1605-06*
49¼″ × 39¾″ Borghese Gallery, Rome

Bellori tells us that Caravaggio painted this picture for Cardinal Scipione Borghese, one of the leading patrons of the day, and that 'the head of Goliath, which David holds by the hair, is a self-portrait'. A description of the Villa Borghese published in 1650 says that David represents 'il suo Caravaggino' – 'Caravaggio's boy'.

The Caravaggisti

Caravaggio founded no school of painting, but his striking style inspired a host of followers from all over Europe, who adapted his bold design and strong tonal contrasts to their own ends.

It is perhaps ironic that although Caravaggio had no pupils he was, in fact, the most influential Italian painter of the 17th century. His works were copied and imitated not only in Rome and Naples, the scenes of his greatest activity, but all over Italy, and the foreign artists who flocked to Rome took his style back to their own countries.

It is easy to see why Caravaggio's work should have made such an enormous impact. It was bold and exciting, conveying an intense sense of physical presence that made the work of most contemporary painters seem anaemic. And – superficially at any rate – it was easy to imitate, for although Caravaggio's work is in many ways complex and subtle, the most immediately striking feature of his style – the use of boldly lit figures emerging dramatically from dark shadows – was simple to grasp.

In view of Caravaggio's unsavoury personality, it is hardly surprising that few of his followers knew him closely. Of those who did, the most outstanding was Orazio Gentileschi. He developed a personal and poetic version of Caravaggio's style, without the master's intensity of feeling, but with a stately grace of his own that makes him at his best one of the most attractive Italian artists of his generation. Like most of Caravaggio's followers, Gentileschi did not continue working in a Caravaggesque style throughout his career; he ended his days in England, painting in a light, decorative manner.

Among the host of other Italian Caravaggisti working in Rome were Carlo Saraceni, a painter of great distinction and sensitivity who painted a replacement for Caravaggio's *Death of the Virgin* (p.34) after it had been rejected by the church of

Lauros-Giraudon

Soldiers Playing Dice
(above) Le Valentin (1591-1632) was a French Caravaggesque painter who settled in Rome. His most famous works are barrack-room scenes – a subject which became popular in France.

Scala

Biblioteca Parucelliana, Florence

Caravaggio
(left) The artist's bold and dramatic style of painting inspired many followers – although most of them copied the obvious aspects of his style without his intense spirituality. This portrait, by Ottavio Leoni, shows the painter's brutto di volta – *'ugly face'.*

Réunion des Musées Nationaux

The Rest on the Flight into Egypt
(right) Orazio Gentileschi's style was more muted than Caravaggio's, and his sense of colour and concern with fabrics was probably the most developed of Caravaggio's followers. He did several versions of this painting, which was inspired by Caravaggio's treatment of the same theme (p.25).

Musee des Beaux Arts, Tours

The Chastisement of Cupid
(right) Bartolommeo Manfredi (c.1587-1620/1) was an early follower of Caravaggio. No signed painting of his exists and several paintings now attributed to him were once thought to be by Caravaggio, including this one. This painting is not typical of Manfredi who is better known for his genre scenes.

Charles H. and Mary F.S. Worcester Collection

The Art Institute of Chicago

Visit to Sicily
(right) Caravaggio was the only major 17th-century artist to work in Sicily. This may account for the long-lasting, though unspectacular, impact he had on the island's native artists.

H. Lütticke/Zefa

Louvre, Paris

S. Maria della Scala, and Bartolommeo Manfredi, who although not such a fine painter occupies an important historical position. It was Manfredi who popularized tavern and guardroom scenes, types that Caravaggio himself did not paint, but which became particularly popular with Northern artists who were visiting Rome. In this way Manfredi played a key role in the expansion and diffusion of the Caravaggesque style.

The painters who took up Caravaggio's style varied enormously in skill and also came from markedly different backgrounds and artistic traditions, so they do not in any way form a homogenous group. Some artists had merely a brief flirtation with the style before developing in completely different directions. The Bolognese painter, Guido Reni, is one example. He is regarded as one of the great representatives of the classical tradition in 17th century art, and the idealistic forms and clear colours of his most characteristic works are the direct opposite of all that Caravaggio stood for. Early in his career, however, he too fell under the hypnotic spell of Caravaggio's art and adopted his bold lighting effects and naturalistic details.

NAPLES: STRONGHOLD OF STYLE

Caravaggio's style went out of fashion in Rome in the 1620s, but it had a longer lease of life in other parts of Italy, not least Naples. Two outstanding Italian artists played major roles in establishing the city as a stronghold of the style. The first was Giovanni Battista Caracciolo, who more than almost any other of Caravaggio's followers saw beyond the superficial characteristics of the master's work to the tragic grandeur at its heart. One of his masterpieces, *The Liberation of St Peter*, was painted for the Chiesa del Monte della Misericordia soon after Caravaggio had executed his huge *Seven Works of Mercy* for the same church, and Caracciolo's noble painting lives up to this exalted company.

Caracciolo's work became lighter and more classical in the 1620s, but the second great representative of Caravaggism in Naples – Artemisia Gentileschi – worked in that style throughout her artistic career. The daughter of Caravaggio's friend Orazio Gentileschi, she had formidable strength of personality, living a life of independence rare for a woman of the time. Many Neapolitan painters were inspired by Caravaggio

Detroit Institute of Arts

Gift of Leslie H. Green

The Royal Collection. Reproduced by Gracious Permission of Her Majesty the Queen

Artemisia Gentileschi (1593-1652/3)
Having worked in Rome and Florence, before settling in Naples, this excellent artist (self-portrait above) was important in disseminating Caravaggio's chiaroscuro and realism. Judith and Holofernes *(left) was her favourite subject.*

Utrecht
(right) Utrecht is the capital of the smallest Netherland state of the same name. It became the northern centre of the Caravaggesque style where Baburen, Honthorst and Terbrugghen worked. As a Catholic centre, Utrecht was more receptive to religious paintings than its Protestant neighbours, and so the influence of Caravaggio prospered.

Puck-Kornetzhi/Zefa

to paint scenes of horrific violence, and Artemisia made something of a speciality of pictures representing the biblical story of Judith beheading Holofernes. Her passion for the theme, which she painted with fierce intensity, has been linked to the events of her life, for when she was 19 she was allegedly raped by the painter Agostino Tassi, who spent eight months in prison before being acquitted. Artemisia was tortured during the course of the legal proceedings, and it has been suggested that her suffering at the hands of men led her to choose as her favourite subject a scene of a woman triumphing bloodily over a man.

Also active in Naples was the great Spanish-born painter Jusepe de Ribera, whose early works are in a style heavily indebted to Caravaggio, but made distinctive by particularly rough and vigorous brushwork. (Most of the followers of Caravaggio preferred a fairly smooth and impersonal surface.) Ribera was a highly respected and influential artist and his work helped to spread the Caravaggesque style to Spain.

The style also travelled to other parts of Europe. It lingered longest in Sicily (which Caravaggio visited), Utrecht in Holland and Lorraine in France, surviving into the 1650s in all three places. There was no one outstanding Caravaggesque artist produced in Sicily, but three fine Dutch painters who had worked in Rome established

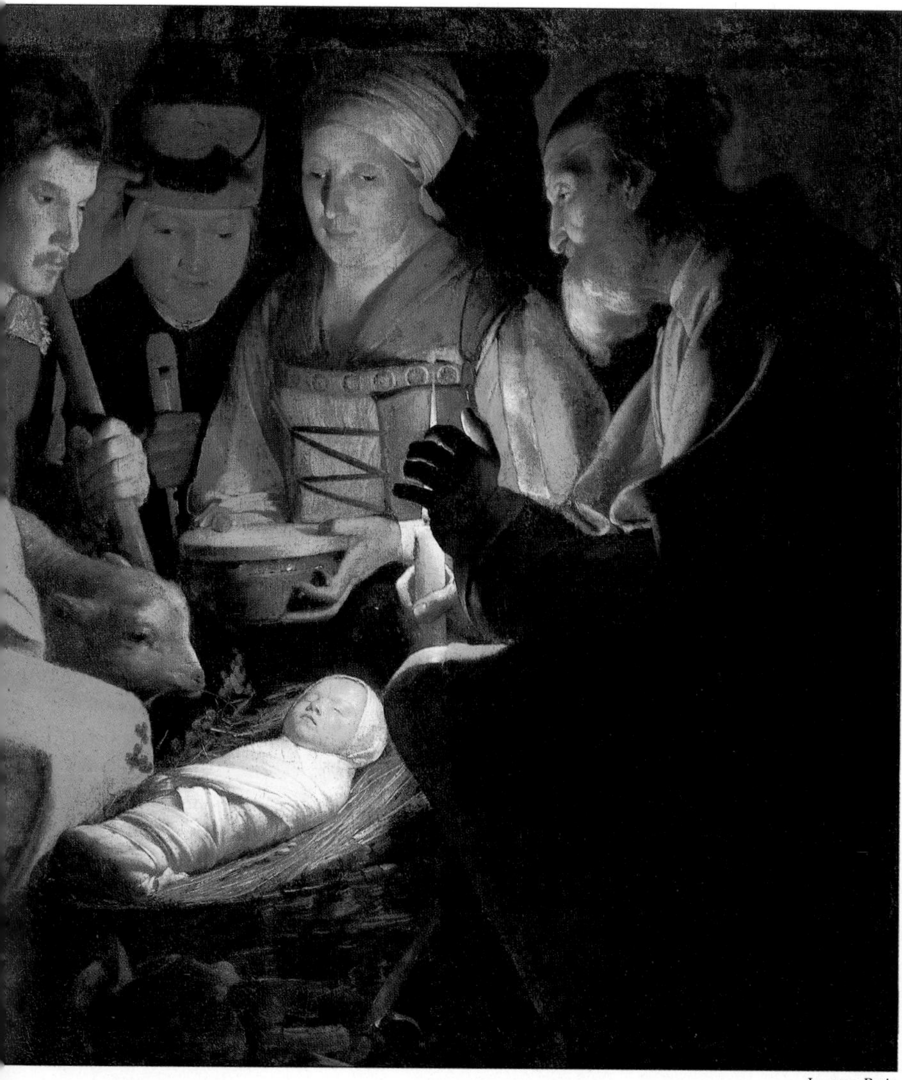

Réunion des Musées Nationaux

Louvre, Paris

this reflects the bias against Caravaggio and his followers that became standard in art criticism from about the middle of the 17th century. In 1633, Caravaggio was described by the Spanish painter and writer Vincenzo Carducho as an 'evil genius' who was a pernicious influence on other artists, and in 1642, the Italian painter and biographer Giuseppe Baglione, who had personally known and hated Caravaggio, denounced him in terms that contain the seeds of much later criticism: 'Some people consider him to have been the very ruination of painting, because many young artists, following his example, simply copy heads from life without studying the fundamentals of drawing and the profundity of art and are satisfied with colour values alone. Thus they are incapable of putting two figures together or of composing a story because they do not understand the high value of the noble art of painting.' The Victorians' strong aesthetic and moral revulsion against Caravaggio's work was best expressed in the vituperative writings of the critic John Ruskin.

It is only in the 20th century that there has been a reassessment of Caravaggio and his followers and artists such as Georges de La Tour and Artemisia Gentileschi have taken their place among the great names of European painting.

Utrecht as the Northern centre of the style: Dirck van Baburen, Gerrit van Honthorst and Hendrick Terbrugghen. Of these, Honthorst was the nearest to Caravaggio in spirit; in Italy he became known as Gherardo delle Notti (Gerard of the night scenes) because of his skill with dramatically lit nocturnal subjects, but he worked in this style only in the early part of his career. Later, for about the last 30 years of his life, he became a successful court portraitist.

Adoration of the Shepherds
(above) Georges de La Tour (1593-1652) is perhaps the greatest of the Caravaggisti. As he never travelled, the source of his style remains a problem, although it may have been gained via Utrecht painters like Honthorst.

THE GREATEST OF THE CARAVAGGISTI

It was in Lorraine that Caravaggio's influence bore its greatest fruit, in the work of the enigmatic painter Georges de La Tour, now thought of as the most inspired reinterpreter of Caravaggio's style. Whereas many of the Caravaggisti took up the violent aspects of the master's work, La Tour evoked the profoundly meditative mood and deep spirituality of his last great paintings. He often used a single candle as the source of illumination, treating the effects of its glow with exquisite sensitivity, and his figures have astonishing grandeur and serenity. Amazingly enough, La Tour is not known to have visited Italy and it is a matter of conjecture how he came by his knowledge of Caravaggio's style.

La Tour fell into obscurity after his death and

Christ before the High Priest
(right) Gerrit van Honthorst (1590-1656) probably influenced de la Tour. Both painted dramatic scenes lit by a single candle, as here, and their colouring, using warm reds and browns, is not dissimilar.

The National Gallery, London

A Year in the Life 1600

By 1600, Caravaggio's criminal exploits were already on record but the papal authorities were more concerned with the dangerously unorthodox ideas of Giordano Bruno. In Britain, Elizabeth I was dealing firmly with the Earl of Essex while her cousin, James VI of Scotland, became the target of the 'Gowrie Conspiracy'.

Giordano Bruno was about 52 years old when he was burnt alive in the Campo di Fiori in Rome on 17 February 1600. Bruno had joined the Dominican order in Naples at 15 and had fled in 1576 after being charged with heresy. Thereafter he wandered over most of western and central Europe as a scholar-writer with his own brand of magical philosophy which urged a return to the purity of hermetic 'Egyptian' religion. In 1591 Bruno returned to Italy at the invitation of a noble Venetian, Giovanni Mocenigo, intending to win there support for his new theocracy. Instead he found himself denounced to the Inquisition by his host and by May the following year embarked on eight years of trial and imprisonment at Rome. His final refusal to admit the heretical nature of his beliefs led inevitably to his execution.

Victoria & Albert Museum, London

Bulloz

Bibliothèque L' Arsenale, Paris

Werner Forman Archive

AISA

An East India Company Officer
(above) In December 1600, Elizabeth I granted an initial charter to a group of merchants for a trade monopoly in the East Indies. Thus began the East India Company, whose commercial activities were concentrated mainly in India. To protect them against the French colonialists in the 18th century, the British were forced to establish local government and a standing army in the subcontinent.

Heretical Dominican
(right) Giordano Bruno was a hermetic philosopher dedicated to Copernican science and Renaissance magic. He was also ultimately anti-Catholic, seeing Christianity as a weak imitation of the one true 'Egyptian' religion of the ancients. At the same time he asserted that the sun was at the centre of our solar system in an infinite universe. Bruno was burned alive as a dangerous heretic on 17 February 1600.

Henri IV of France was more concerned with secular matters. In 1600 he was involved in a punishing campaign against Savoy and contracted his second marriage – to Marie de' Medici, the niece of the Grand Duke of Tuscany.

FOOLHARDY FAVOURITE

England was much concerned with a rumoured Spanish invasion of Ireland in support of the Catholic Irish under the Earl of Tyrone. In 1599 Queen Elizabeth attempted to restore authority with an army led by the Earl of Essex, but the favourite dissipated his forces, ignominiously agreed to a truce, and dashed back to London. Tyrone was in arms again in 1600, but Elizabeth's new Lord Deputy, Mountjoy, brought to the task a patience and systematic approach that the headstrong Essex lacked. The Irish were kept on the run, even during the winter and a series of forts was constructed which gradually reduced the territory under Tyrone's control.

While Mountjoy prospered, his friend Essex lay in deep disgrace. He had believed that his hold over the Queen would lead her to forgive the Irish fiasco and his unauthorised return, but Elizabeth, encouraged by Essex's numerous enemies, was furious. Essex was imprisoned until June 1600 when a special tribunal heard him abjectly confess his faults, but he was not allowed his liberty until August. He bombarded the Queen with lover-like letters, and they probably met – but only to quarrel. This was disastrous for Essex who was deeply in debt and dependent on Elizabeth's bounty. Above all, his lucrative

'. . . the play's the thing'
(left) Shakespeare's Hamlet, obliged to revenge his father's murder, is one of literature's great tragic heroes. The play, written around 1600, is as immediate in its impact today as it was then.

Earl of Essex
(below) Elizabeth I's favourite, overplayed his hand in 1600. The next year he paid with his life for not realizing that the caprices of a favoured courtier were not appropriate when it came to matters of state.

AISA

Peter Paul Rubens and Jan Brueghel/The Archduke Albert of Austria

Giancarlo Costa

National Maritime Museum, London

Archduke Albert at the Battle of Nieuwpoort
(above and below) The peace-loving Archduke, joint-ruler of the Netherlands with his wife Isabella, sister of Philip III of Spain, was obliged to fall in with his brother-in-law's plans to invade the Dutch republic in 1599. The Dutch counter-attacked the next year with a hard-won victory at Nieuwpoort in Flanders, but were forced to retreat due to heavy losses.

Fotomas

10-year monopoly of sweet wines was to expire in the autumn and when it was evident that the Queen would not renew it Essex realised he was a ruined man, so becoming more unstable than ever. 'He shifteth from sorrow and repentance to rage and rebellion so suddenly as well proveth him devoid of good reason or right mind', wrote an eyewitness. Nevertheless, the Earl had a formidable number of retainers and a large popular following. In February 1601 he made a fatally confused attempt to raise the City of London which led to his trial for treason and subsequent execution.

Equally grim was the 'Gowrie conspiracy', an affair still shrouded in mystery. There had been a history of bad feeling between James VI of Scotland and the Ruthven family, and to make matters worse, the crown owed them a large sum. The King invited young Alexander Ruthven hunting and after the kill they both rode back to Gowrie House, dined and then withdrew together to an upper room. Suddenly, James' attendants heard cries for help, broke into the apartment to find James and Alexander apparently grappling and slew the young man. His elder brother, Lord Gowrie, was also killed in the scuffles that followed. The official version was that James had foiled an assassination attempt and was overpowering Ruthven when his attendants arrived. But James' physical cowardice was notorious and there were several inconsistencies in his story. Whatever the truth, the 'conspiracy' was a catastrophe for the Ruthvens: the bodies of the two brothers were gibbetted and quartered and the very name of Ruthven abolished.

Marriage by Proxy
(left) Henry IV, the first Bourbon King of France, divorced his first wife, Marguerite of Valois, in 1599 after a childless marriage. He was then free to wed Marie de' Medici, daughter of the Grand Duke of Tuscany, whose dowry included the cancellation of all French debts to Florence. Their union was solemnized by proxy in Florence Cathedral the following year. Her father stood in for the absent bridegroom who was deeply embroiled in negotiations over the French possession of Saluzzo in Savoyard territory. Henry had agreed to take Bresse from the Duke of Savoy in return for Saluzzo but Spain, concerned about the maintenance of her 'road' north through Europe to the Netherlands, offered to support the Duke if he rejected the agreement – this he foolishly did on 7 August. Henry immediately mobilized his troops and successfully invaded Savoy while the Spanish did nothing for their new ally. By November, Henry felt sufficiently confident of the military situation to journey to Lyons, where he met his new bride for the first time, and the month-old marriage was finally confirmed.

Scala

Peter Paul Rubens/The Marriage by Proxy/Louvre, Paris

DD Velasquez

1599-1660

The greatest of all Spanish painters, Velázquez enjoyed a career of continual success. Precociously gifted, he was producing masterpieces while still in his teens, and at the age of 24 became a favourite painter of Philip IV. The King had an extraordinarily high opinion of Velázquez's personal qualities as well as of his talent as a painter and awarded him many prestigious court appointments. Yet his work remained little known outside Spain.

Velázquez excelled primarily as a portraitist, painting sitters ranging from the King to the pathetic court dwarves with unmatched human sympathy. He produced superb work in other fields, however, notably in his rare excursions into painting the nude or historical subjects. Because Velázquez spent so much time on his court appointments, and as he was a slow worker, his surviving output is fairly small.

The King's Favourite

Born in Seville, Velázquez enjoyed enormous success at the court of Philip IV in Madrid. The King was so overwhelmed by his skills that he was reluctant to be portrayed by any other painter.

Key dates

1599 born in Seville
1611 apprenticed to Pacheco
1617 accepted as master painter
1618 marries Pacheco's daughter
1623 becomes court painter to Philip IV
1628-29 befriends Rubens on his visit to Spain
1629-31 visits Italy
1634-35 paints *Surrender of Breda*
1649 returns to Italy
1651 back in Spain
1656 paints *Las Meninas*
1659 knighted
1660 dies in Madrid

Diego Rodríguez de Silva y Velázquez was born in Seville and baptized there a few days later on 6 June 1599, the first of seven children of Juan Rodríguez de Silva and his wife Jerónima (née Velázquez). There was noble blood in the family, but his parents were comfortably off rather than rich. Diego, as was not uncommon in Spain, took his mother's name rather than his father's, and later usually signed himself, using a variant spelling, Diego Velasquez.

Seville at this time was the most prosperous city in Spain. It was the main port for the trade with the Americas that had given Spain huge wealth by its silver imports and it had a very cosmopolitan atmosphere. Seville was also a major cultural centre, and when the young Diego – who is said to have excelled at every subject he studied – showed particular interest in painting, his parents could have chosen from several talented painters to become his teacher. There are two main early sources of information on Velázquez's life and they are in conflict as to the boy's training. Francisco Pacheco, who was certainly Velázquez's main master, claimed that he alone taught Velázquez, but the painter and writer Antonio Palomino said that the boy was first sent to study with Francesco de Herrera the Elder. Herrera was infamous for his violent temper (which caused his son, another painter of the same name, to flee from home) and if Velázquez did study with him it can only have been for a very short period.

Fotomas

British Museum

Aisa

Velázquez's birthplace *(left) Velázquez was born in Seville in Andalusia, then Spain's wealthiest city and an important cultural centre.*

St John on Patmos *(above) Velázquez's master, Pacheco, was so impressed by his pupil that he copied one of his compositions (p.50).*

A SYMPATHETIC TEACHER

Velázquez's contract of apprenticeship with Pacheco was made out in September 1611 for a period of 'six years dating from 1 December of the preceding year' (the reason for the backdating is not known). Pacheco was a mediocre painter, but in some ways Velázquez's parents could not have made a better choice. He was a highly cultured man – a poet as well as a painter – and his house was a meeting place for artists and scholars. It must have been a stimulating atmosphere, and Velázquez himself grew up to be a man of broad

Scala

Prado, Madrid

The Adoration of the Magi (detail)
(left) This is one of Velázquez's early religious works, painted when he was only 20. It is thought to include a portrait of his 17-year-old wife, Juana – his master's daughter – and the couple's first child.

cultural interests, as is shown by the inventory of his library drawn up after his death. As a teacher, Pacheco seems to have been the opposite of Herrera – sympathetic, receptive to new ideas, and generous enough in spirit to acknowledge openly that Velázquez was a far better painter than himself: 'I consider it no disgrace for the pupil to surpass the master.'

On 14 March 1617, soon after completing his apprenticeship, Velázquez was examined and accepted as a *maestro pintor de ymagineria* (master painter of religious images), which was the highest class of painter. Just over a year later, on 23 April 1618, Velázquez married Pacheco's daughter Juana; the bride not quite 16 and the groom not quite 19. Pacheco wrote 'I married him to my daughter, moved by his virtue, his integrity, and good parts and by the promise of his natural and great talent.' There is no known portrait of Juana by Velázquez, but it is highly likely that she was the model for some of his early paintings, such as *The Immaculate Conception* (p.56). The couple had two daughters, Francisca, who was born in 1619, and Ignacia, who was born in 1621 and died in infancy.

Velázquez soon made a reputation in Seville with works like *The Adoration of the Magi* (left) which already showed great mastery. In April 1622 he visited Madrid, partly to see the palace of the Escorial with its magnificent art treasures, but also

The royal court at Madrid
(below) Once he had established his reputation in Seville, Velázquez journeyed to Madrid, with the object of painting the new King and seeing the treasures of the Escorial.

Arxiu Mas

Municipal Museum, Madrid

An eye-catching portrait
(right) During his stay in Madrid Velázquez painted a portrait of the distinguished poet, Luis de Góngora. The picture proved a great success and brought him to the King's attention.

Museum of Fine Arts, Boston (Marie Antoinette Evans Fund)

because he had conceived the bold plan of trying to gain an opportunity of painting a portrait of the new King, Philip IV, who had been crowned in the previous year. He was unsuccessful in his second aim, but he did paint a portrait of the great poet Luis de Góngora before his return to Seville. His work must have made a considerable impression in Madrid, for in 1623 he was recalled to the capital by the Count-Duke of Olivares, chief minister to the King and, like Velázquez, a Sevillian. Velázquez was ordered to make a portrait of the King, and this was judged such a success that he was made one of the court painters. More than that, the King was so pleased that he decided that from now on no-one but Velázquez should paint his portrait. At the age of 24 he had suddenly become the most prestigious painter in Spain.

The Spanish court was a place of stiff etiquette, but Velázquez made such an impression on the young King (he was six years younger than the painter) that they enjoyed a remarkably warm relationship. 'The liberality and affability with which Velázquez is treated by such a great monarch is unbelievable', wrote Pacheco. 'He has a workshop in the King's gallery to which His Majesty has the key, and where he has a chair, so that he can watch Velázquez paint at leisure, nearly every day.'

ROYAL FAVOUR

Such favouritism aroused the jealousy of the other court artists, who accused Velázquez of being capable of painting only heads. To answer the slander, Philip ordered Velázquez and three other artists to paint a picture of *The Expulsion of the Moriscos,* a grand multi-figure composition. Velázquez won the competition, but unfortunately his painting – his first work on an historical subject – was destroyed in a fire in 1734.

To rub salt into his rivals' wounds, Philip made Velázquez Usher of the Chamber on 7 March 1627,

Zefa

Roman sojourn
(above) In August 1629 Velázquez satisfied a long-cherished desire to visit Italy. He journeyed to Naples and Venice, but spent about a year in Rome where he studied the art that had inspired generations of artists before him. According to his friend, Jusepe Martínez, he returned 'much improved' by his endeavours.

'The God of Wood'

Velázquez lived in a golden age for Spanish art and among his contemporaries was the man who is often regarded as his country's greatest sculptor, Juan Martínez Montañés (1568-1649). He was known as *'el dios de la madera'* ('the god of wood') because of his superlative skills as a carver. Most Spanish sculpture of the time was painted in naturalistic colours and much of the work of Montañés (who spent almost all his life in Seville) was painted by Velázquez's master, Pacheco.

Aisa

Seville Cathedral

Scala

Prado, Madrid

Sculptor of dignity
(left and above) Velázquez painted Montañés' portrait when the sculptor came to Madrid to make a clay bust of Philip IV. Velázquez must have seen in the sculptor a kindred spirit, for his work, although powerful and realistic, always has great dignity. Montañés' moving crucifix, made c.1603, seems to have had a profound impact on the young artist.

Rubens in Madrid
(right) In 1628, the famous Flemish painter Peter Paul Rubens arrived in Madrid on diplomatic business. He stayed for nine months, during which time he painted several portraits of the Spanish royal family and befriended Velázquez. Rubens was impressed by the modestia *of Velázquez's paintings, and the latter does not seem to have been in the least overwhelmed by Rubens' ebullience and formidable artistic energy. Together they made frequent trips to the Escorial where they indulged their love of Titian.*

The Villa Medici
(right) This remarkably spontaneous oil sketch shows the rambling gardens of the Villa Medici, where Velázquez stayed during his first visit to Rome. He painted this view on a return visit some 20 years later, when the Villa was undergoing extensive repairs. On this occasion Velázquez ordered casts to be made of some of the finest pieces from the Villa's impressive collection of classical sculpture.

Aisa

Prado, Madrid

Bridgeman/Christies, London

Rubens/Self-Portrait

the first of a succession of court posts extraneous to his duties as a painter. These appointments were to the benefit of Velázquez's worldly status but to the detriment of his art, for although the positions held grand titles such as Supervisor of the Works of the Palace, they wasted his time in trivial bureaucratic matters. He carried out his duties efficiently, however, and seems to have been temperamentally suited to them; one of the few personal comments we have on him from a contemporary (the Venetian painter Marco Boschini) describes him as 'a courtly gentleman of such great dignity as distinguishes any person of authority'.

In 1628-29 the great Flemish painter Rubens visited Spain on diplomatic business. Pacheco and Palomino both record that Rubens and Velázquez became friends, and another contemporary stated that Rubens 'confessed that Velázquez was the greatest European painter'. Together they went to the Escorial, and as Palomino wrote, 'they both took especial delight in admiring the many and admirable works of genius in that sublime structure, in particular the original paintings of the greatest artists to flourish in Europe. These provided a new stimulus to Velázquez and revived the desire he had always had to go to Italy to inspect and study those splendid paintings and sculptures which are the torch that lights the way for art, and the worthy objects of veneration.'

Velázquez was given official permission from the King to travel to Italy on 26 June 1629 and in August he set sail from Barcelona to Genoa. In his absence he was to receive 'the same salary and other payments as now'. From Genoa, Velázquez went to Venice, then passed through Ferrara and Cento (where he may have met the great Italian painter Guercino) on his way to Rome, where he stayed for about a year. He then went to Naples, which at the time was a Spanish possession. The greatest painter living there was another Spaniard, Jusepe de Ribera, and Velázquez almost certainly

Mazo/The Artist's Family/Kunsthistorisches Museum, Vienna

The Pope's reward
(above) Pope Innocent X presented Velázquez with a gold medal in appreciation of the portrait of 'extraordinary merit' which the artist had made of him in 1650 on his second visit to Rome (p.65).

The fruits of old age
(left) Velázquez's grandchildren were a source of great pride and a consolation to him in his later years.

met him. By January 1631 he was back in Madrid. Many of the works that Velázquez is known to have made in Italy are lost (including a self-portrait and various copies of famous works of art), but two major paintings survive from the period – *Joseph's Coat* and *The Forge of Vulcan*. They show how his mastery of figure composition increased under the influence of classical art and the great Renaissance masters.

A FEAST OF PAINTINGS

The next two decades were the most fruitful period of Velázquez's career. He painted numerous portraits of the King and the royal family (Philip had allowed no-one else to portray him while Velázquez was in Italy), including a breathtaking series of equestrian portraits; he did his finest work in religious painting and also painted his only surviving female nude; and he created one of the world's supreme masterpieces of history painting – *The Surrender of Breda* (pp.58-9). The incomparable series of portraits of court fools ('El Primo' and Sebastián de Morra are shown on pp.60-61) also dates from this middle period. All the while his life went on in a completely unruffled manner, punctuated by such events as the marriage of his daughter Francisca to his outstanding pupil Juan Bautista Martínez del Mazo in 1633, or by his advancement to some new royal office, but without any kind of external drama.

It is possible that Velázquez made a short trip to Italy in 1636 but the evidence is inconclusive. Certainly the country held a powerful attraction for him, and in November 1648 he set off on

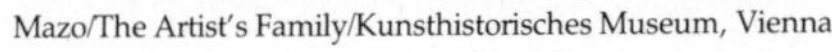

El Esclavo

The painter Juan de Pareja (c.1610-1670) was a *mulatto* – someone of mixed white and black (in his case Moorish) parentage – and has become known to posterity by the nickname *El Esclavo* (the slave). The 18th-century biographer, Antonio Palomino, stressed that Pareja was Velázquez's slave but, because of confusion with another painter of the same name who was clearly a free man, Palomino's statements were dismissed as fanciful embroidery on the facts and historians accorded Pareja the status of servant and assistant. In 1983, however, a document was published showing that Palomino was right all along, for on 23 November 1650, in Rome, Velázquez granted Pareja his freedom.

Aisa

Provincial Museum of Huesca

another extended visit. Palomino records that he 'was sent by the King to Rome as Ambassador Extraordinary to Pope Innocent X to buy works of painting and sculpture and to have casts made of the more famous Greek and Roman sculptures'. As on his first journey 20 years earlier, Velázquez visited several cities (including Naples, where he saw Ribera), but it was once again in Rome that he stayed longest. His reputation had preceded him and he was honoured with membership of the Academy of St Luke.

In 1650, the year of this great triumph, King Philip sent a whole series of letters to his ambassador in Rome to urge Velázquez to return to Madrid, and a surprising documentary discovery, published in 1983, has shown he may have had reasons other than those connected with art for wanting to prolong his stay in Italy. From the document we learn that a widow called Martha had borne Velázquez's illegitimate son, Antonio. The child was described as a babe in arms in October 1652 and Velázquez was back in Madrid by June 1651, so he may never have seen his son. He applied for permission to return to Italy in 1657 but was refused, and it is tempting to speculate that Martha and Antonio were as much on his mind as the glories of Italian art. Nothing is known of the fate of mother or child.

Arxiu Mas

A last journey
(left) In 1660, Velázquez travelled to the Isle of Pheasants on the Franco-Spanish border, to make arrangements for the marriage of Philip IV's daughter to King Louis XIV of France. The wedding came as the conclusion to peace negotiations which had been conducted throughout the previous year. (A monument, still standing on the 'Isle', commemorates the Peace treaty.) The demands of the journey took their toll on the elderly Velázquez and on his return to Madrid his health rapidly deteriorated.

Aisa

Prado, Madrid

The Baptism of Christ (c.1667)
(left) Little is known of Pareja's own work as a painter. Palomino says that he painted portraits that could be mistaken for Velázquez's, but most of his few surviving works are of religious subjects in a rather flamboyant style that is very different from his master's. This work shows that artistically he borrowed freely from several sources, drawing heavily on his familiarity with Venetian masters.

The Calling of St Matthew (1661)
(above) This painting includes a self-portrait of Pareja on the far left. Pareja has clearly based it on the celebrated portrait that Velázquez made of him in Rome in 1650 (p.64). On the basis of this work, it seems highly unlikely that Pareja's portraits could have been confused with his master's. They have none of the qualities of incisiveness or immediacy so typical of Velázquez's many great works.

This skeleton in the cupboard may have posthumously dented Velázquez's reputation as a model of moral rectitude, but it seems to have done nothing to disturb his calm life in Madrid. He suffered a blow in 1654 when his daughter died, but otherwise he went serenely about his painting and his court duties.

In 1652 he was appointed to the most prestigious of all his court posts, *Aposentador Mayor* (King's Chamberlain), but he craved the crowning glory of a knighthood, and the almost interminable process to secure this dragged on throughout the artist's final years. Philip had to obtain special permission from the Pope (Alexander VII) before he could dub Velázquez a Knight of the Order of Santiago on 28 November 1659. The self-portrait of Velázquez in his *Las Meninas* (p.66), shows him with the cross of the order on his breast.

AN EXHAUSTING MISSION

On 8 April 1660 Velázquez left Madrid for the Isle of Pheasants on the border between Spain and France to make preparation for the meeting of the King with Louis XIV of France, who was to be married to Philip's daughter the Infanta Maria Theresa. He returned to Madrid on 26 June, exhausted by the work and the travelling. On 31 July he took to his bed in his apartments in the royal palace complaining of a fever, and he died on 6 August, 'mourned by all', as Palomino related, 'and not least by the King'. He was buried in the church of S. Juan Bautista, which was destroyed in 1811, leaving no trace of his mortal remains. His grieving widow survived him by less than a week.

An Eye for Truth

A skilful portraitist, Velázquez possessed an extraordinary ability to convey the inner life of his sitters. Ignoring the external trappings of rank, he communicated their essential humanity.

Velázquez's art seems to unfold with the same calm and serious dignity as his life. There are no abrupt changes in his style, but rather a gradual perfecting of his incomparable skills. His late works are entirely different from those of his youth, but his progress was so subtle that it is notoriously difficult to date his paintings on grounds of style alone. *The Rokeby Venus* (pp.62-3), for example, was traditionally considered one of Velázquez's very last works until documents proved it was in a Spanish nobleman's collection in June 1651 and was therefore probably painted before the artist left for Italy in 1648.

A SLOW WORKER

Velázquez seems to have been a slow worker and because so much of his time was taken up with court duties his output was small. Less than 150 surviving paintings are attributed to him and even making allowances for those that have perished in the intervening centuries it is doubtful if the original total was much above 200. This is a small number for a working life of over 40 years – an average of about one picture every two months.

National Gallery of Scotland, Edinburgh

National Gallery, London

Old Women Frying Eggs
(above) Painted only a year after Velázquez had completed his apprenticeship, this bodegón *is a fine example of the artist's ability to faithfully record the features of his models and invest them with dignity while avoiding idealization.*

Saint John the Evangelist on the Island of Patmos
(left) In this early religious work, Saint John records his vision of the Woman of the Apocalypse. The Saint is usually shown as an old man, but Velázquez portrays him as a youth, who resembles the characters depicted in the bodegones.

Francisco Pacheco, Velázquez's master, taught him to 'go to nature for everything', and in his treatise *The Art of Painting* he recorded the diligence with which his young pupil followed his instructions: 'He used to bribe a young country lad who served with him as a model to adopt various attitudes and poses, sometimes weeping, sometimes laughing, regardless of all difficulties. And he made numerous drawings of the boy's head and of many other local people and thereby he gained assurance in portraits.'

Assurance is indeed an outstanding feature of Velázquez's precocious genius, for while he was still in his teens he was painting pictures that display complete technical mastery. Most of his early works were either religious paintings, or what are known as *bodegones.* The Spanish word *bodegón* translates as something like 'tavern' or 'low eating house', but it has come to be applied to kitchen or similar scenes that feature prominent still-life details. Such pictures enjoyed great popularity in Spain, but no other artist painted them with the mastery of Velázquez. His biographer Palomino says that he won 'great fame and well-deserved esteem' by such works, and that when 'some people remonstrated with him because he did not paint more serious subjects

Arxiu Mas

Academia Bellas Artes des Fernando, Madrid

Study for a Head 1643-5
(left) Few authenticated drawings by Velázquez still exist, but this sensitive study for a portrait of Cardinal Borja is thought to be by the artist. He apparently painted a portrait of Borja when he occupied the see of Toledo.

Philip IV c.1626
(right) This sombre image of the Spanish king stands in stark contrast to earlier royal portraits, which had emphasized costume and regalia. The sitter's Habsburg jaw and fleshy lips are portrayed with an almost brutal honesty.

The Spinners c.1656-8
(below) This picture illustrates the contest between Pallas Athene and Arachne, who challenged the goddess to a weaving competition, and who was changed into a spider when she lost. The two women are shown in the background tapestry.

Scala

Prado, Madrid

with delicacy and beauty, in emulation of Raphael of Urbino, he politely replied that he preferred to be the first in that kind of coarseness than second in delicacy'. *The Waterseller of Seville* (p.57) is the finest example of these low-life subjects.

A CHANGE OF DIRECTION

With his move to Madrid in 1623 the direction of Velázquez's work changed. From now on portraiture became his main concern; he gave up *bodegones* entirely, and religious, historical and mythological subjects occupied a diminishing part in his output. His way of handling paint changed too. In his early work it is thick and richly textured; sometimes it has a leathery appearance and sometimes, as in the clouds in *The Immaculate Conception* (p.56), it is rather like ricotta cheese. Under the influence of the paintings he saw in the royal collection, however, particularly the work of Titian, Velázquez's touch became lighter and broader, and he began to prefer rather bare settings without the superbly painted still-life elements that had been such a feature of his work in Seville. Gradually, Velázquez completely subordinated detail to overall effect, so that in his late works space and atmosphere are rendered

Scala

Prado, Madrid

COMPARISONS

Papal Portraits

There is a long tradition of great papal portraits, for the head of the Catholic Church has always been in a position to attract the outstanding artists of the day. In 1543, Pope Paul III specially summoned Titian to Bologna to paint his portrait. Velázquez was also honoured with papal commissions, and painted his remarkable portrait of *Innocent X* (p.65) while in Rome in 1650. The tradition has been continued into modern times by Francis Bacon, whose tormented visions are often nourished by art of the past.

Scala

Museo Capodimonte, Naples

Titian (c.1485-1576)
Pope Paul III
(left) The three-quarter length and three-quarter angled view of the sitter that Titian adopted here became something of a convention in papal portraiture. Velázquez admired Titian's work, and his own Innocent X *shows a great debt to the Venetian master.*

Francis Bacon (b.1909)
Pope I
(right) In the 1950s Francis Bacon painted a whole series of variations on Velázquez's Innocent X. *His work shares with that of Titian and Velázquez a superb mastery in the handling of paint, but his horrific imagery inhabits an entirely different world.*

Aberdeen Art Gallery

Scala

Prado, Madrid

The Buffoon Juan de Calabazas or Calabazillas
(above) The gourds in this portrait ('calabazas' in Spanish) identify the sitter as Juan de Calabazas, a buffoon in the service of Philip IV. Since he died in 1639, the picture probably dates from the late 1630s, around the time when Velázquez was painting his portraits of dwarves. Calabazas was not a dwarf himself, but the fact that he seems to be crouching in a corner gives him the air of an outcast.

with astonishing vividness, but the individual forms when looked at closely dissolve into blurred brushstrokes. As Palomino said of his work 'one cannot understand it if standing too close, but from a distance it is a miracle'.

ESSENTIAL HUMANITY

This sense of truth is a feature not only of Velázquez's technical skills, but also of his characterization, for his paintings are not only extremely life-like but also full of compassion and understanding for his fellow men. As a court painter he was, of course, concerned with conveying status, but he always looks beyond external trappings to the human mystery beneath. Thus Philip IV, for all his royal dignity as the ruler of the world's greatest empire, remains a man who has lived and suffered like everyone else. And even the pitiful court dwarves preserve a divine spark. We feel that all his sitters have a soul and that to Velázquez they are all worthy of respect because they are equal in the eyes of God.

This marvellously democratic spirit and ability to empathize with his subjects is also apparent in Velázquez's other work. In *The Surrender of Breda* (see pp.58-9), for example, he avoids any of the

allegorizing of which Rubens would have made such a show and concentrates instead on the human drama of the situation. The Spanish victor receives the keys of the town from his defeated opponent with what is surely the most superb gesture of magnanimity in the history of art.

SPONTANEOUS WORKING METHODS

We know little about Velázquez's working methods. There are very few drawings by him (although those that do exist reveal the hand of a master draughtsman), so it is probable that he usually worked directly onto the canvas. He often altered a picture as he went along; although it may need X-rays to make this clearly visible, the evidence can sometimes be seen by the naked eye when an overpainted passage shows through a superimposed layer that has faded with age. Palomino says that he used exceptionally long brushes, but there seems nothing out of the ordinary about the one he is holding in *Las Meninas* (p.55). The number of good copies that exist of many of Velázquez's pictures suggests that he ran a busy studio. Several of his pupils and assistants are known by name, but only his son-in-law Juan del Mazo and his slave, or assistant, Juan de Pareja achieved any kind of independent identity.

With a few exceptions such as the portrait of *Innocent X* in Rome (p.65), Velázquez's paintings remained little known outside Spain until after the Napoleonic Wars, as the country was isolated from the rest of Europe. From the early 19th century, however, the subtlety and technical freedom of his work made him a great hero of progressive artists, especially Manet.

A momentary glance
(above) It is difficult to know how to interpret Calabazas's grin and unfocused eyes. The full ambiguity of the court jester's changing expression is conveyed by Velázquez's deliberately vague and hazy rendering of the buffoon's somewhat pathetic and shy face.

Prince Philip Prosper, 1659
(right) Velázquez probably painted this moving portrait of the prince on the child's second birthday. The frailty of the short-lived young boy is evident in his sickly pallor, and in the amulets to ward off the evil eye that adorn his costume.

TRADEMARKS

Character Impressions

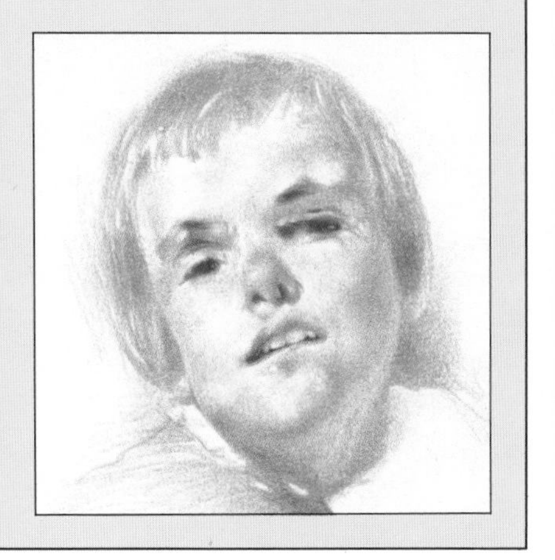

In Velázquez's paintings fascination with character is always paramount. Models and sitters are painted truthfully and without idealization. Sometimes his desire to capture fleeting expression led the artist to paint faces in a very loose, free manner, so that on close inspection of the canvas they appear to be out of focus.

Kunsthistorisches Museum, Vienna

THE MAKING OF A MASTERPIECE

Las Meninas

The title *'Las Meninas'* (which means 'the maids of honour') dates only from the 19th century and sheds little light on the meaning of the picture. This complex work shows Velázquez painting in his studio surrounded by members of the royal household. Alternative explanations have been advanced to explain exactly what is going on: that Velázquez was painting the King and Queen (reflected in the mirror) when he was interrupted by the little Infanta and her companions, or vice versa. By putting himself in the picture, Velázquez was asserting his own importance, although he may be expressing some guilt about his presumption by showing two Rubens sketches on the wall which depict the downfall of mortals who have the temerity to attempt to challenge the Gods in the arts.

Arxiu Mas

Prado, Madrid

Arxiu Mas

The young Infanta
(left) 17th-century observers described Las Meninas *as a portrait of the Infanta Margarita with her attendants, and the princess does seem to be the focus of attention – perhaps she is even being cajoled into sitting for her portrait.*

The Infanta Margarita (1656)
(right) In the same year as he painted Las Meninas, *Velázquez painted another portrait of the young princess which conveys the stiffness and formality of the Spanish court.*

Kunsthistorisches Museum, Vienna

Mari Bárbola
(right) On the right stands Mari Bárbola whom Palomino described as 'a dwarf of dreadful appearance'. Her lumpish features present a pathetic contrast with the delicacy of the little princess.

Arxiu Mas

The painter at work
(below) The artist's hands – rendered by a few swift brushstrokes – seem to move rapidly from palette to canvas. The Cross of the Order of Santiago on his breast is a later addition, as it was not awarded to Velázquez until 1659.

Royal reflections
(below) The image of the King and Queen in the mirror has prompted much speculation. It may represent the monarchs who are sitting for their portrait, or it could be a reflection of a portrait hanging on the opposite wall. This idea is supported by the red drapery and half-length format, but no such work by Velázquez is documented. Whatever the source of the reflection, the mirror is a clever device to suggest the presence of the King and Queen without actually showing them as part of the main picture.

Giraudon

Arxiu Mas

'. . . to paint a whole group on such a large scale . . . that requires a most unusual gift.'

Kenneth Clark

Gallery

Velázquez began his career painting in a solid, almost sculptural manner that bears witness to his close study of nature. The Immaculate Conception and The Waterseller of Seville are two of the finest examples of this style. After he moved to Madrid as court painter in 1623 he continued to base his work on nature, but his means of expression grew

The Immaculate Conception *c.1618*
53¼″ × 40″ National Gallery, London

This radiantly beautiful painting was probably one of the first official commissions Velázquez received after becoming a master painter in 1617. The Immaculate Conception, representing the doctrine that the Virgin was conceived free of Original Sin, was enormously popular in Spain, and Velázquez follows a formula that was later codified by his master Pacheco in his treatise, The Art of Painting. *Pacheco stipulated that the Virgin should be shown as a girl of 12 or 13, with her hands on her breasts or in prayer, and that the moon on which she stands should be a crescent (a symbol of chastity originally associated with the virgin goddess Diana) and have its points downwards. The model for the Virgin may have been Velázquez's wife, and in the companion picture of St John the Evangelist (p.50), also in the National Gallery, it was once thought that he may have represented himself.*

so subtle that in the 40 years that separate these two pictures from The Infanta Margarita his technique had developed to a breathtaking freedom and fluency. Las Meninas is the supreme example of his ability to capture a sense of living reality by painting exactly what the eye sees rather than what the mind knows to exist.

It is as a portraitist that Velázquez is most famous, and his pictures of Juan de Pareja, Innocent X and the court fools show that his ability to depict character has never been surpassed. As The Surrender of Breda and The Rokeby Venus demonstrate, however, his genius could be just as original in the fields of history painting and the nude.

The Waterseller of Seville
c.1620
41½" × 31½" Wellington Museum, London

Velázquez made his name with bodegones *(low-life scenes involving food and drink) and this has always been recognized as the finest of them, making an image of grandeur and gravity from a commonplace event. The virtuosity of his technique is seen particularly in the drips of water on the large jug in the foreground, which seem almost palpable. This was one of scores of pictures looted from the Spanish royal collection by Joseph Bonaparte (Napoleon's brother) that were recovered after his defeat by the Duke of Wellington at the Battle of Vittoria in 1813. The Duke wished to return them to Ferdinand VII of Spain, but the grateful King insisted that Wellington should keep them. Wellington's collection thus includes three paintings by Velázquez and many other Spanish pictures.*

Scala

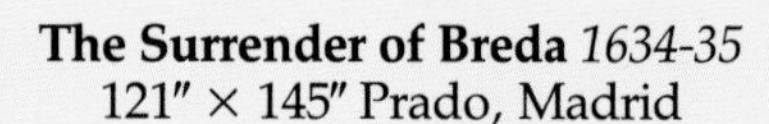

The Surrender of Breda *1634-35*
121″ × 145″ Prado, Madrid

The Dutch town of Breda, a strategically important stronghold in the struggle against Spanish oppression, was captured by the Spaniards in June 1625 after a ten-month siege. Velázquez's painting, which shows Count Justin of Nassau handing over the key of the town to the Spanish leader Ambrogio Spínola, was one of a series of 12 paintings by court artists commemorating the military successes of Philip IV's reign that formed part of the decoration of the new Buen Retiro Palace in Madrid. Both commanders were dead by the time Velázquez painted the picture (he had known Spínola, but had never seen Justin) and he relied on descriptions and engravings to recreate the event. Considering this, the sense of actuality he achieved is astonishing, for the picture is so convincing pictorially and psychologically that it seems like vivid reportage. Spínola became famous for his clemency at Breda (the terms of surrender were remarkably lenient) and his unforgettable gesture as he places his hand on his deafeated opponent's shoulder expresses perfectly his chivalrous spirit. X-rays show that Velázquez altered the painting as he went along; the superb horse at the right was an afterthought. The forest of pikes on this side of the painting, which contrasts with the bedraggled looking Dutch weapons on the left, has given the picture its popular Spanish title 'Las Lanzas' (The Lances). Two years after Velázquez finished this incomparable masterpiece, the Dutch recaptured Breda.

Scala

The Court Fool 'El Primo' *1644*
42″ × 32½″ Prado, Madrid

Velázquez made four celebrated portraits of court fools but this is the only one that can be dated precisely, for it is known to have been painted in 1644 when Velázquez accompanied Philip IV to Fraga in Aragon to put down a revolt. The jester Diego de Acedo, known as 'El Primo', was also employed in clerical work – hence the book.

Scala

The Court Fool Sebastián de Morra *c.1644*
41¾" × 32" Prado, Madrid

Like other monarchs, Philip IV kept dwarves and idiots for his amusement. Velázquez's portraits of these small human beings show his sympathy, for each is treated as an individual and there is no suggestion of caricature. Sebastián de Morra came to the court in 1643 and this portrait was probably done soon after.

The Rokeby Venus *c.1648*
48¼" × 69¾" National Gallery, London

Velázquez's only surviving painting of the female nude takes its name from the fact that in the 19th century it was owned by the Morritt family of Rokeby in Yorkshire. Paintings of the nude are rare in Spanish art because they were generally considered to be obscene, but Velázquez is recorded as painting others, which are now lost. The Rokeby Venus *is first recorded as belonging to a Spanish nobleman Don Gaspar Méndez de Haro in June 1651 and it is probable that Velázquez painted it shortly before he left for his second visit to Italy in 1648. It was Titian who popularized the subject of Venus at a mirror attended by Cupid and the Venetian influence in The Rokeby Venus is so strong that some critics think it may have been painted in Italy and shipped back to Spain. In the 18th century the painting belonged to Goya's intimate friend the Duchess of Alba, and it is likely that it provided some of the inspiration for Goya's* Naked Maja *(possibly representing the Duchess), which led him into trouble with the Inquisition. In 1914 a suffragette demonstrator badly slashed* The Rokeby Venus *in the National Gallery; it has been excellently restored, but the marks of the attack are still visible on close examination.*

Juan de Pareja *1650*
30″ × 25″ Metropolitan Museum of Art, New York

Velázquez painted this portrait of his slave in Rome because he felt he needed practice before painting the one of the Pope (opposite). It caused a sensation in 1970 when it was sold at Christie's in London from the Earl of Radnor's collection for £2,310,000; no painting had ever previously fetched even £1,000,000 at auction.

Scala

Pope Innocent X *1650*
55″ × 47½″ Galleria Doria Pamphili, Rome

One of Velázquez's best-known works this is universally regarded as a supreme masterpiece of portraiture, as much for the breathtaking handling of paint as for its psychological penetration. Acknowledging how brilliantly Velázquez had captured his character, the Pope said the portrait was 'troppo vero' *('too truthful').*

Arxiu Mas

Las Meninas (The Maids of Honour) *1656*
125″ × 109″ Prado, Madrid

Luca Giordano called Las Meninas *'the Theology of Painting' because 'just as theology is superior to all other branches of knowledge, so is this the greatest example of painting'. Modern critics and artists agree; a poll of them in* The Illustrated London News *in August 1985 voted Las Meninas 'the world's greatest painting'.*

The Infanta Margarita in Blue *1659*
50″ × 42″ Kunsthistorisches Museum, Vienna

Because the King and his courtiers usually wore sombre clothes, Velázquez often had to paint in muted tones, but when the occasion arose, he showed he was a superb colourist. The Infanta Margarita is the little princess in Las Meninas*. With a picture of her brother (p.53), it was the last one Velázquez finished.*

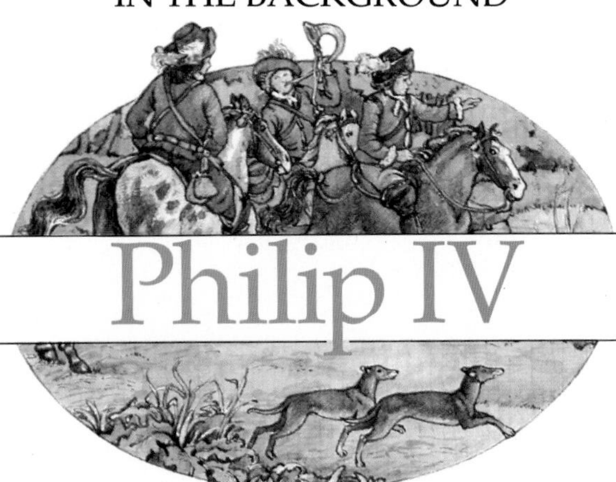

Philip IV

The reign of Philip IV was one of the strangest periods in Spanish history – an age of contradictions, as traditionally Catholic Spain tried to come to terms with the changing face of 17th-century Europe.

For artists, such as Velázquez, the reign of Philip IV was a golden age, for the King was a patron of the arts like few others in Spanish history. Philip spent vast fortunes on art and entertainment and, under his care, Spanish culture blossomed to a remarkable extent. First and foremost, of course, there is the work of Velázquez himself. But then there is a long list of literary giants, such as the poets Góngora and Quevedo and the playwrights Calderón and Lopé de Vega, all of whom produced their greatest work in Philip's reign. Playwrights did especially well, for Philip had an ardent love of the theatre and his demand for new plays seemed insatiable. But the crowning achievement of his patronage was the magnificent palace of *Buen Retiro* (Good Retreat) in Madrid, a beautiful mansion containing some of Velázquez's

Patron of the arts
(right) As a patron of the arts, Philip IV was hugely successful. But unfortunately for his crumbling empire, he was an unfit and weak ruler.

A ruthless politician
(below left) Gaspar de Guzman, Count of Olivares was the power behind the throne. Different in every way from the King, he was determined to return Spain to its former glory.

Velázquez. National Gallery, London

Scala

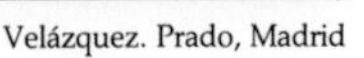

Velázquez. Prado, Madrid

Arxiumas

Lavish entertainment
(above) When the future Charles I of England visited Madrid in the hopes of securing the hand of Philip's sister, Maria, the capital burst into bloom and the recent law banning the wearing of finery was suspended. Philip and Olivares pretended to be in favour of the marriage in order to extract concessions from Charles, and lavishly organized fiestas such as the one shown here.

finest paintings and a superb collection of art treasures.

Yet while Spanish art was flourishing, Spain itself was withering. The once mighty Spanish Empire was being undermined from within and from without, as subject peoples rebelled against the harsh yoke of Spanish rule, and rival powers sniped at Spain's numerous and scattered provinces.

EMPIRE IN DECLINE

Almost continuous war throughout Philip's reign saw the total eclipse of Spain as a dominating military force in Europe. Defeat after shattering defeat in the Thirty Years War (1618-48) so undermined Spain's prestige that she slipped from the very hub of European power politics to its outer rim. The Empire, though still vast, became a hollow sham and the Crown was barely able to impose its will on its many subject peoples. Indeed, Spain effectively gave up any pretence to control its Dutch provinces in the north of Europe, and even parts of the Spanish heartland were lost. Portugal broke away to become independent forever, Catalonia was lost to the French for many years and Roussillion permanently.

The Spanish economy, already in tatters at the beginning of Philip IV's reign, had all but disintegrated by its end. Long years of almost unrelieved war, shrinking revenues, appalling mismanagement of the economy, combined with a drastic decline in agricultural production, brought the country to its knees, financially and socially. Future revenues were pledged to pay off current debts; the currency swung sickeningly between rampant inflation and stultifying deflation; and the Crown itself went bankrupt over and over again.

Heightening the tension was the extraordinary extravagance of the Crown. While the people of Spain time and time again shouldered the vast cost of the war effort with crippling taxes, the court was on a spending spree. As the Empire burned, the court fiddled, danced and played on a lavish scale. In Madrid, few months would pass by without the staging of some dazzling spectacle or another. Many aristocrats as well as peasants had been reduced almost to penury and such extravagance was bound to cause resentment.

THE KING'S CHARACTER

At the heart of these contradictions was the King himself and his chief minister for 30 years, Don Gaspar de Guzman, Count of Olivares. On the surface, Philip IV was ever the child of pleasure. From an early age, Philip was besotted by the theatre and as he grew older, was equally enthusiastic about 'adult' pleasures. One was hunting. He was a brilliant horseman and would happily spend 12 hours in the saddle. In one year, apparently, he is believed to have 'bagged' 150 boars, 400 wolves and 600 deer. Just as tireless was his pursuit of women. He had many mistresses and is known to have fathered at least 30 illegitimate children – his success in the royal bed was not quite so impressive and the lack of a suitable heir was one of the most unsettling factors of his reign. His mistresses were treated well for a while but once his interest waned, or the

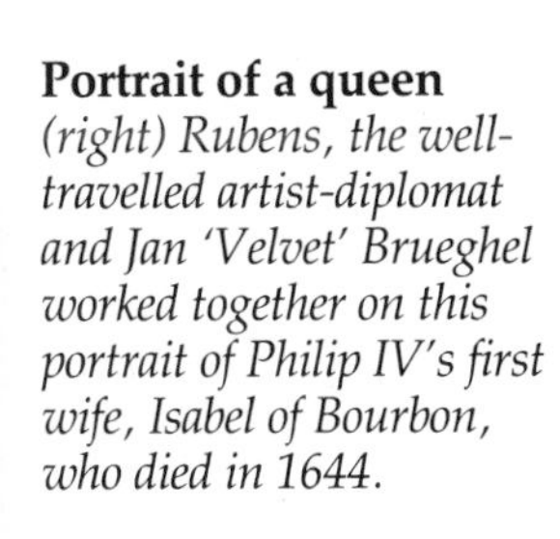

Velázquez. National Gallery, London

Portrait of a queen
(right) Rubens, the well-travelled artist-diplomat and Jan 'Velvet' Brueghel worked together on this portrait of Philip IV's first wife, Isabel of Bourbon, who died in 1644.

The boar hunt
(left) One of Philip IV's favourite pastimes was hunting. Here Velázquez portrays the King and his minister, Olivares meeting the charge of the boar.

Rubens & Jan Breughel. Prado, Madrid/Aisa

Valázquez. Prado, Madrid/Giraudon

Son and heir
(above) Prince Baltasar Carlos, shown here at six dressed as a hunter, was the only child from the marriage of Isabel and Philip. His death in 1646 left Spain without an heir.

A favourite mistress
(right) The actress La Calderona was a mistress of the King. Their son, John of Austria, was handsome, popular and ambitious. He eventually became Prime Minister.

unfortunate woman became pregnant, she would be expected to tactfully withdraw from the world and enter a convent (to repent her sins?).

All these happy pursuits left Philip very little time for the serious business of monarchy. Paperwork bored him; issuing instructions frightened him; and only ceremonials, with their theatrical aspect, gave him any pleasure. Olivares would often admonish him for letting business slip – though, in reality, he was glad to encourage the King's laxity, for it increased his own power.

Yet behind this frivolous, weak-willed exterior lay a deep melancholy, a melancholy caught by Velázquez in his later portraits of Philip IV. Despite his antics he seemed to feel, all too acutely, the duties and responsibilities of kingship – so acutely, indeed, that he felt himself inadequate in the face of them. Rather than working at a task for which he was clearly unfit, he preferred to hand over control to a more authoratitive figure, first Olivares; then, when Olivares' disastrous policies finally caught up with him, Olivares' nephew Don Luis de Haro. The King only took control himself for the last few years of his life. He was constantly wracked by guilt about his lack of assertiveness and would, now and then, attempt to make up for his 'sinful' behaviour. But the attempts were short-lived, and the old uncertain lassitude would soon creep back.

A DOMINANT MINISTER

Perhaps the key to his vacillation was the Count of Olivares. For 22 years, Olivares dominated both Philip himself and Spanish politics. He was a remarkable figure who presented a complete contrast to the King. Their relationship had begun when Philip was barely 11 years old – Olivares having skilfully manoeuvred himself into the position of Gentleman of the Bedchamber to the

Arxiumas

Arxiumas

young prince. Olivares (18 years older than Philip), soon came to dominate the boy's life, exerting his powerful personality over Philip and virtually running his life for him. It was Olivares who encouraged the King in his pursuit of pleasure, perhaps to distract him from running the country, thereby leaving it to the Count. It was Olivares who encouraged the extravagant displays in Madrid. Indeed, the palace of Buen Retiro, begun when the country was in desperate straits financially, was actually Olivares' doing. Perhaps he hoped to enhance Spain's prestige by showing that all was well in the capital.

In direct contrast, Olivares pursued the imposition of direct control over all parts of the Empire with great vigour. His pursuit of the war effort was unrelenting, and he would impose taxes mercilessly to pay for this, and the extravagance of the Crown. To support these measures, he

A magnificent palace
(above) The King ordered the construction of the Buen Retiro Palace, which was later furnished with priceless art treasures.

War-torn Spain
(below) Wars and weak leadership saw the end of Spain as a power.

Painter of the people
(right) While Velázquez was court painter, Murillo, a fellow Sevillian, captured the 'real', poverty-stricken face of Spain.

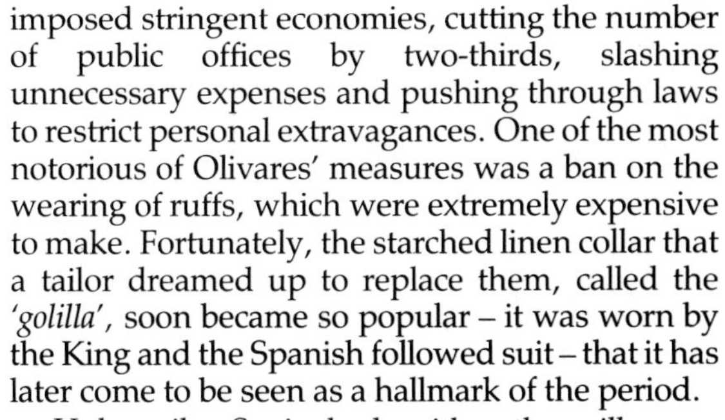

imposed stringent economies, cutting the number of public offices by two-thirds, slashing unnecessary expenses and pushing through laws to restrict personal extravagances. One of the most notorious of Olivares' measures was a ban on the wearing of ruffs, which were extremely expensive to make. Fortunately, the starched linen collar that a tailor dreamed up to replace them, called the *'golilla'*, soon became so popular – it was worn by the King and the Spanish followed suit – that it has later come to be seen as a hallmark of the period.

Unhappily, Spain had neither the willpower nor the unity to make Olivares' aggressive policies work. With the exception of a few dramatic successes, such as the fall of Breda to Spinola, the rest was a catalogue of setbacks – culminating in the loss of Portugal and Catalonia in two separate revolutions in one week.

EBBING POWER

It was all too much for Olivares. In January 1643, the Count was forced to resign and retired to the country, a broken man, to die a few years later. Thereafter, Spain's fortunes took a slight upturn as events in other countries told in her favour and the King fathered a son and heir. But Philip never really came to grips with lifting his crumbling empire from the doldrums. And as he saw Spain's time as a major power gradually ebb, he looked on with a melancholy air. In 1661, Haro died. So did Philip Prospero, Philip's young heir – and the son born a few days later, Carlos, was grotesquely deformed. Four years later, the melancholy, guilt-wracked King was dead, and 'in all the . . . capital, there was not one person who shed a tear'.

Snayers. Prado, Madrid/Aisa

Munich Antiqua Pinacoteca/Arxiumas

A Year in the Life 1656

In 1656 Velázquez was to immortalise the Spanish royal court in his masterpiece *Las Meninas,* just as Spain's greatness was coming to an end. Meanwhile in Republican England, which was once again threatening Spanish domination of the seas, there were rumours of a possible Coronation — that of King Oliver I.

By 1656 Spain was in a state of exhaustion, having been at war for decades, latterly competing against France in a struggle for European supremacy. She had been unable to subdue the rebellious Portuguese, her economy was ruined and most worrying, there was a considerable falling-off of bullion supplies from the Americas. She was able to carry on fighting only because France was intermittently weakened by the civil wars of the Fronde. In 1656 the French were prepared to make peace, but Spanish pride made it impossible. By 1656 Republican England, led by the Lord Protector Oliver Cromwell, had become a formidable foe. An English expedition had snatched Jamaica from the Spaniards in 1655, making Spain's declaration of war in February 1656 a formality. In September a detachment of Admiral Blake's fleet under

Giancarlo Costa

John Casimir
(above) In December 1655 the Polish King returned to his kingdom, overrun by Swedish, Russian and Cossack armies, only to be defeated outside his capital of Warsaw in July 1656.

Robert Harding Picture Library

Splendid gardens
(above) André le Nôtre began work in 1656 on the formal gardens of Vaux-le-Vicomte, which inspired those of Versailles.

Brett Froomer/The Image Bank

St Peter's Square
(right) Bernini, the great Baroque architect and sculptor, began work on the design of St Peter's Square, Rome, in 1656. His unique contribution was the free-standing colonnades, a detail of which is seen here.

Captain Richard Stayner, made off with 600,000 pieces of eight off Cadiz, a bitter blow to the already tremendously impoverished Spanish exchequer.

CROMWELL CURBS THE COMMONS

The poet Edmund Waller suggested that Cromwell should be given 'a royal sceptre made of Spanish gold'. Many people agreed, and the Parliament that met in September moved slowly towards offering the crown to the Lord Protector. But republican feeling remained strong, as the publication of James Harington's *Oceana* indicated. This book contained a scheme for a republican constitution on Venetian lines. The philosopher was shrewd enough to dedicate it to the Lord Protector and to attribute the founding of his ideal state to a thinly disguised Cromwell, 'Olphaeus Megaletor'. Eventually, after months of agonizing, Cromwell refused the proferred crown, though he took the opportunity to increase his powers as Lord Protector and introduce a second chamber (similar to the abolished House of Lords) as a check on the House of Commons.

This conservative measure was prompted by the difficulty Cromwell found in controlling the Commons. A particularly sensational example occurred in the case of James Nayler, a young Quaker, who had made many converts. The effects of his personal magnetism turned his head (whether he became literally insane is not so clear). In October 1656 he entered Bristol to a rapturous welcome from followers chanting 'holy, holy, holy', the scene quite evidently being a conscious re-

Marshal Turenne
(right) France had been racked by the civil wars of the Fronde since the end of the Thirty Years' War in 1648. Turenne, arguably the greatest French general of his day, had initially supported the Frondeurs. *The third war however saw him fighting his old confederate the Prince de Condé who had allied with Spain. Though successful in the previous four campaigns, Turenne's royalist army, defeated at Valenciennes in 1656, won ultimate victory two years later.*

Edimages

Black Death
(left) The plague epidemic that decimated Naples and Genoa in 1656 formed part of a massive outbreak that had afflicted Seville in 1648 and moved inexorably through Europe.

Museo Nationale de San Martino/Giraudon

Saturn's rings
(right) The Dutch physicist and astronomer Christiaan Huygens not only observed and described the rings of Saturn during the winter of 1655-6 but by the end of the year 1656 he had also invented the pendulum clock.

Science Photo Library

enactment of Jesus' entry into Jerusalem. For this 'horrid blasphemy' Nayler was arrested and tried by the House of Commons itself, despite the fact that the House had never possessed any such judicial competence. Cromwell did his best to obtain a merciful verdict, but the Commons was in full cry, and decreed that the unfortunate Nayler should be pilloried, branded, have his tongue bored with a hot iron, paraded through Bristol and whipped, and then be imprisoned indefinitely. It was therefore not surprising that Cromwell should want to curb an assembly that behaved so intemperately and so confidently flouted his authority.

In Europe Cromwell's name was becoming respected. Even the warrior-King, Charles X of Sweden, was angling for an English alliance, despite the remote scene of his operations. In 1655 Charles had plunged into Poland, aiming to make himself king or, more realistically, to strengthen Sweden's grip on the southern shore of the Baltic. Together with his ally, Frederick William of Brandenburg, their joint forces were victorious in a great three-day battle at Warsaw in the last days of July 1656. But by the end of the year the Holy Roman Empire and Russia had come to Poland's assistance. Frederick William, eventually to be known as 'the Great Elector', by a judicious change of sides secured international recognition for his sovereignty over East Prussia, which he had previously held under the suzerainty of the Polish crown. In time, Frederick William's Hohenzollern descendants would make themselves kings of Prussia, and ultimately build this inheritance into an imperial Germany ruled by the Hohenzollern Kaisers until 1918.

Versailles, Chateau/Lauros-Giraudon

Stockholm Drottningholm Palace/Giancarlo Costa

Amedeo Vergani/The Image Bank

Skilful diplomat
(above left) During 1656 Cardinal Mazarin opened negotiations with Spain on territorial and dynastic issues. This was to result in the Treaty of the Pyrenees and the eventual marriage of the Infanta of Spain to Louis XIV.

Anarchy in Istanbul
(left) For two months of 1656 Istanbul was the scene of mob violence incited by unpaid Ottoman soldiers returned from Crete. The struggle with the Venetians for mastery of the Aegean had drained Turkish coffers.

Warsaw taken
(above) Charles X of Sweden with his ally the Elector of Brandenburg succeeded in crushing the Polish army outside Warsaw in July 1656. Despite this Charles was eventually to gain nothing from his Polish invasion.

Scala

Van Dyck: Self-portrait with Endymion Porter (detail)/Prado, Madrid

Ant van Dyck

1599-1641

Anthony Van Dyck was one of the most successful portraitists in the history of art. His dazzling images of the court of Charles I were enormously influential in his own time, and determined the course of English portraiture for the next 200 years. Van Dyck was brilliantly precocious, and although greatly influenced by Rubens – with whom he worked in Antwerp – he was to a large extent a self-taught artist.

In 1621 Van Dyck travelled to Italy, where he made his name painting portraits of the Genoese aristocracy. On his return to Antwerp six years later, he was showered with commissions and was appointed court painter to the Archduchess Isabella. In 1632 Van Dyck was summoned to England by Charles I and made chief painter to the King. But despite such success, Van Dyck never achieved his ambition to be a history-painter.

The Gallant Portraitist

Van Dyck had a career of glittering international success. In Italy, Flanders and England he perfected a style of aristocratic portraiture that became the model for court artists all over Europe.

Key Dates

1599 born in Antwerp

1609 apprenticed to Hendrick van Balen

1618 enters Antwerp Guild; begins working with Rubens

1620/21 first visit to England

1621 travels to Italy and settles in Genoa

1624 commissioned to paint the *Madonna of the Rosary*

1627 returns to Antwerp

1632 settles in England

1635 paints *Charles I in Three Positions*

1640 marries Mary Ruthven

1641 birth of daughter; Van Dyck dies in London

Wallace Collection

A romantic image
(above) Van Dyck was obviously proud of his good looks and painted several flattering self-portraits. Here, aged about 25, he portrays himself as the shepherd Paris, who in Greek mythology awarded Venus the golden apple in the celestial beauty contest that started off the Trojan War.

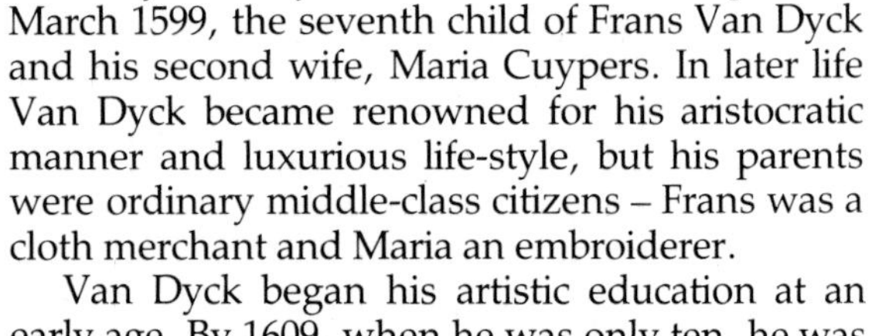

Anthony Van Dyck was born in Antwerp on 22 March 1599, the seventh child of Frans Van Dyck and his second wife, Maria Cuypers. In later life Van Dyck became renowned for his aristocratic manner and luxurious life-style, but his parents were ordinary middle-class citizens – Frans was a cloth merchant and Maria an embroiderer.

Van Dyck began his artistic education at an early age. By 1609, when he was only ten, he was already apprenticed to the successful figure-painter, Hendrick van Balen. But Van Balen made little impression on his young pupil, since Van Dyck was exceptionally precocious. He was also highly ambitious, and by 1615 he had left Van Balen and set up his own studio in Antwerp, together with two young assistants. In doing so Van Dyck was breaking the rules of the painters' guild, for an artist was not supposed to sell his work until he had officially qualified as a master.

During Van Dyck's early years, the artistic scene in Antwerp was dominated by Rubens. His genius posed an obvious challenge to an aspiring young painter, and it may have been Rubens' presence in Antwerp that prompted Van Dyck's early bid for independence and recognition. It was probably also the example of Rubens, who was equally successful as a diplomat and man of court,

Giraudon-Lauros

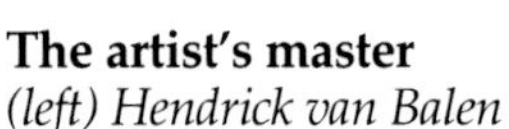

The artist's master
(left) Hendrick van Balen (1573-1632) specialized in religious and mythological paintings and was a respected figure who often collaborated with other artists.

His Grace the Duke of Norfolk KG, Arundel Castle

A noble patron
(above) Thomas Howard, 2nd Earl of Arundel, was one of the greatest patrons and collectors of his day – surpassed in England only by Charles I. Here Van Dyck shows Howard with his wife, Aletheia.

Bernard G. Silberstein/Rapho

Success in Genoa
Van Dyck was in Italy from 1621 to 1627. He visited various cities, but had his greatest success in Genoa with his superb portraits of the aristocracy. Genoa was (and still is) one of the most important ports in Italy, and in the 17th century had a flourishing school of painting, enriched by visitors such as Rubens and Van Dyck.

National Gallery, London

Assistant to Rubens
Van Dyck was one of many artists who worked with Rubens and may have had a hand in this picture. The foliage and fruit are perhaps by Frans Snyders, an eminent specialist in animals and still-life.

that encouraged Van Dyck to adopt an aristocratic manner, and to cultivate the image of himself as a man of sophistication and refinement. Van Dyck also emulated Rubens' painting style, which he mastered with astonishing facility.

EARLY SUCCESS AND FAME

On 11 February 1618, Van Dyck was registered as a master in the Antwerp Guild of St Luke. Later that year he entered into his first direct association with Rubens. Rubens was designing a set of tapestries, showing the story of the Roman consul Decius Mus, for a patron in Genoa. He seems to have engaged Van Dyck to execute the full-scale cartoons after his *modelli*, giving Van Dyck an unparalleled opportunity to observe the master at work. Two years later, when he was just 21, Van Dyck was named as Rubens' chief assistant in the major commission to provide ceiling paintings (now destroyed) for the Jesuit Church in Antwerp, a sure sign of his professional success.

However, despite Van Dyck's prodigious talent and ambition, Rubens does not appear to have felt threatened by the young artist, although it has been suggested that it was Rubens who encouraged Van Dyck to specialize in portraiture – a field in which Rubens had relatively little interest. In fact Rubens clearly supported Van Dyck in his career and openly admired his talent, owning nine of Van Dyck's works.

By 1620 Van Dyck's reputation in Antwerp was firmly established. So it was not surprising that when, in July of that year, the influential Countess of Arundel passed through the city on her way to visit Italy, and sat to Rubens for his portrait of her, her secretary, Francesco Vercellini, wrote to the Earl of Arundel in London about the progress of the work, and added a note about the young painter. 'Van Dyck is still with Signor Rubens' he reported, 'and his works are hardly less esteemed than those of his master; he is a young man of twenty-one, and his father and mother, who are very rich, live in this city; so that it will be difficult for him to leave these parts, all the more as he sees the good fortune that attends Rubens.'

The letter suggests that the Earl was keen to procure Van Dyck's services and, despite Vercellini's reservations, Van Dyck was clearly tempted by the prospect of a visit to England. By November 1620 he had arrived in London, where he was to stay for the next three months.

This brief stay was important for Van Dyck, as he established connections with two of England's leading collectors: the Earl of Arundel himself, and his wealthy rival, the Duke of Buckingham. Van Dyck carried out commissions for both men, painting a portrait of the Earl and producing a fine history painting for the Duke. He also had access to their remarkable collections, which were especially rich in the works of the Venetian Old Masters, whom Van Dyck particularly admired – the Earl of Arundel owned 36 paintings by Titian and the Duke had a large collection of works by Veronese. Van Dyck could have seen a few such works in Antwerp but there is little doubt that his experience of these collections strengthened his enthusiasm for Italian art, and helped influence his decision to travel to Italy the following year.

On 16 February 1621, Van Dyck was granted a payment of £100 for a 'special service' he had carried out for the King, James I. It is not known what this payment was for but, following his experience in Rubens' workshop, he may have been engaged in making tapestry designs for the King's new factory at Mortlake. It seems clear, however, that the King wanted to keep Van Dyck in his service, for on 28 February he was granted a pass to travel for eight months, as 'His Majesty's Servant'. A few days later he returned to Antwerp.

THE ITALIAN PERIOD

Van Dyck stayed in Antwerp until the autumn. Then, on 3 October 1621, he set off for Italy, heading first for the wealthy city of Genoa, probably on the advice of Rubens who had been impressed by the city during his own Italian tour. It was here that Van Dyck began his career as portrait-painter to the aristocracy. He had painted a few portraits in Antwerp, and had begun to move away from the stiff formality of conventional Flemish portraiture. Now, under the renewed influence of Italian art, and with the example of Rubens' Genoese portraits before him, his style expanded dramatically and he began to create portraits of unparalleled sophistication and refinement: one such was his *Portrait of Elena Grimaldi* (p.82).

Van Dyck was very much at home in the magnificent *palazzi* of his aristocratic patrons and the 17th century biographer Bellori described Van Dyck on his arrival in Italy by saying 'His manners were those of a lord rather than an ordinary man, for he had formed his habits in the studio of Rubens, amongst noblemen. He was also proud by nature, and anxious for fame, and in addition to his rich clothing he wore plumes in his hat and chains of gold across his chest, and accompanied himself with servants.'

A Master's Influence

Van Dyck is sometimes loosely referred to as Rubens' pupil, but he was in fact already a highly accomplished artist when he began working for the master in 1618. Nonetheless, Rubens' style exerted an enormous influence on Van Dyck. Many of Van Dyck's early paintings were copies or variants of Rubens' compositions, and the former imitated the latter's work so brilliantly that there is sometimes difficulty, even for those familiar with the artists' work, in distinguishing between their hands.

Kunsthistorisches Museum, Vienna

Royal Collection

A fiery mistress
(left) Margaret Lemon, Van Dyck's mistress in England, was acknowledged as a great beauty, but she had a fiery and unstable temperament that was liable to erupt in rages of jealousy. This tenderly erotic portrait is based on a famous picture by Titian, one of the artists Van Dyck most admired, showing a woman in a fur wrap.

National Gallery, London

The Emperor Theodosius Refused Entry into Milan Cathedral
(left) This and the painting above illustrate how difficult it often is to distinguish between the work of Rubens and Van Dyck at the time when they collaborated. Most critics now attribute this picture to Rubens and the smaller version above to Van Dyck, but the verdict is by no means unanimous.

The Emperor Theodosius Refused Entry into Milan Cathedral
(above) There are many differences of detail in the two pictures, but they are very similar in handling. The greater sense of weight and physical substance in the larger version suggests, however, that it is by Rubens, while this free copy, which is rather more elegant, is by Van Dyck.

Friends in Italy
(right) During his stay in Genoa, Van Dyck lived with Lucas and Cornelis de Wael, two friends from Antwerp who had settled in Italy. The brothers were painters, engravers and dealers in art. Van Dyck painted their portrait, from which this engraving by Wenceslaus Hollar is taken.

But Van Dyck's lordly manner did not endear him to his fellow artists. Bellori reports that during a visit to Rome he upset the local community of Flemish artists by refusing to join the festivities which they traditionally organized to welcome newcomers to the city.

Surprisingly, perhaps, and unlike Rubens, Van Dyck did not embark on an extensive sight-seeing tour in Italy. He was a selective traveller and seems to have decided beforehand what he wanted to see – his notebooks record the works of Titian and Veronese and other notable Venetians, together with sketches of street life. But for the most part Van Dyck remained in Genoa, where he found a ready and appreciative market for his portraits regardless of his personal manner.

After a fairly lengthy stay in Italy, Van Dyck returned to Antwerp in the middle of 1627, summoned by the death of his sister Cornelia. The next six years were to be the most successful and productive of his career: he was employed continuously by the Church, and was inevitably in great demand as a portraitist. By May 1630, he had been appointed Court Painter to the widowed Archduchess Isabella, and painted numerous portraits of Isabella and her entourage, modifying the sumptuous style of his Italian portraits to suit the more austere environment of the Brussels court. He also painted mythological works such as the dazzling *Rinaldo and Armida* (p.81), which was acquired by Charles I in 1629. Van Dyck's *Rinaldo*, with its breathtaking echoes of the Venetian masters, was guaranteed to excite an English audience. Italian paintings dominated the taste of English collectors so it must have aroused considerable enthusiasm in London, and probably influenced Charles' decision to ask Van Dyck to

A taste for landscape
(below) A surprising aspect of Van Dyck's genius is revealed in the series of water-colour landscapes he produced in England. They are painted with great freshness and spontaneity and their unaffected simplicity contrasts strongly with the grandeur and formality so typical of his portraits.

British Museum, London

Van Dyck in Italy

The sketchbook that Van Dyck kept during his years in Italy, now preserved in the British Museum, provides a valuable insight into his response to Italian art. Although he travelled to most of the major artistic centres in the country, Van Dyck was unusually selective in the works of art he recorded. Unlike most artists who made the trip to Italy, and in marked contrast to Rubens, Van Dyck had little interest in the art of antiquity and made only one drawing after a classical sculpture. His sketchbook focuses on the works of Venetian High Renaissance artists such as Titian, Tintoretto and Veronese, whose paintings he had particularly admired in the collections of Flemish and English connoisseurs.

Ch.Erath/Explorer

Fotomas

British Museum, London

A visit to Palermo
(left) In 1624, Van Dyck was invited to Sicily by the Viceroy Emmanuele Filiberto of Savoy. In Palermo, the capital city, he painted his biggest religious commission in Italy, an altarpiece for the Oratorio del Rosario.

A venerable artist
(above) In Palermo, Van Dyck met the portraitist Sofonisba Anguissola, who had been the most famous woman painter of her time. She was in her 90s and almost blind, but Van Dyck wrote that her brain was 'most alert'.

England. In due course, early in 1632, no doubt encouraged by the Earl of Arundel, Charles invited Van Dyck to the English court.

PAINTER TO CHARLES I

Despite this royal invitation it is not altogether clear why Van Dyck should have moved to London, since he had established a successful and varied career in Antwerp. But he was clearly attracted by the life of the Court, and Charles, who became King in 1625, had a formidable reputation as a patron of the arts. Rubens described him as 'the greatest amateur of painting among the princes of the world', and he had given Rubens one of his grandest commissions: the ceiling paintings in the Whitehall Banqueting House.

The King certainly treated Van Dyck with extraordinary generosity. He was lodged in a house at Blackfriars at the King's expense, provided with a summer residence at Eltham, and granted an annual pension of £200. On 5 July 1632, he was knighted, and the following year presented with a gold chain worth £110. Bellori gives a vivid description of Van Dyck's life-style in London. According to the biographer, his house was visited

The King's agent
Nicholas Lanier (1588-1666) was Master of the King's Music and was also employed by Charles I as an agent to buy paintings on the Continent. He was himself a talented amateur painter. Van Dyck painted this portrait of him in Antwerp in 1630, and Lanier may well have influenced his decision to settle in London two years later.

Kunsthistorisches Museum, Vienna

by the greatest nobility of the day who, following the King's example, liked to watch him work and pass the time in his company. In his house, 'he kept servants, musicians, singers and fools, and with these diversions he entertained all the great men who came daily to sit for the portraits'.

Van Dyck worked hard for these rewards; the King and his courtiers were demanding patrons. During the nine years he spent in England, Van Dyck painted around 30 large portraits of the monarchs, who had a special landing stage constructed outside his house in Blackfriars so they could visit him more easily by river. He also had an unending stream of commissions from the aristocracy, and his output of portraits during these years was truly prodigious.

Baltimore Museum of Art

Blauel/Gnamm/Artothek

Alte Pinakothek, Munich

Van Dyck was clearly attractive to women. Although not tall he was well-proportioned and according to Bellori was 'blond with a fair complexion.' His name has been romantically linked with a number of his female sitters, and he had an illegitimate daughter, Maria Teresa, whom he honoured in his will. His accepted mistress was the fiery Margaret Lemon who was described by the engraver Hollar as 'a dangerous woman' and 'a demon of jealousy' who caused the most horrible scenes when ladies belonging to London society had been sitting without a chaperone for their portraits. In a fit of jealousy she tried to bite off Van Dyck's thumb in order to prevent him from painting again.

Despite his success Van Dyck did not intend to settle in England. In March 1634, he returned to Antwerp to visit his family, and bought some property near the Château de Steen, the country residence which Rubens purchased the following year. On the death of Rubens in 1640, Van Dyck made repeated trips back to his native town, no doubt anxious to claim his position as the leading painter in Flanders. But events overtook him, and he died in London in 1641.

The English years
(above left and above) After Van Dyck left England at the end of his first brief stay in 1621, he is not known to have had any contact with the English court for another eight years. In 1629, however, Charles I bought his painting of Rinaldo and Armida *(above left), and this splendid work probably inspired the King to tempt Van Dyck into his service. He arrived in England in 1632 and was based there for the rest of his life. But even though he married an English woman, portrayed above as a cellist, he never really settled and kept up his links with the Continent.*

Van Dyck's last years were not without their disappointments. Despite his talent for portraiture Van Dyck maintained the ambition to be a successful history painter like Rubens, and clearly hoped for a large-scale commission from King Charles. In 1639 plans were made for a series of canvases to decorate the Queen's Bedchamber at Greenwich but Van Dyck was not included in the scheme, and the commission was given to Jacob Jordaens, another assistant to Rubens. In January 1641 Van Dyck travelled to Paris, hoping to gain a major commission from Louis XIII who was planning to decorate the principal gallery in the Louvre. Again he was unsuccessful, and by May he was back in London.

MARRIAGE AND DEATH

A brighter note in these final years was Van Dyck's marriage, early in 1640, to Mary Ruthven who was one of the Queen's ladies-in-waiting. But the marriage did not last long as on 9 December 1641, Van Dyck died, his delicate constitution undermined by the unremitting pressure of work. His eight-day-old daughter, Justiniana, was baptized the same day.

Aristocratic Images

Quick to absorb the inspiration and style of the greatest Italian portrait painters, Van Dyck developed his own extraordinary gifts to become one of the most memorable and influential portraitists ever.

During the course of his career Van Dyck revolutionized English portraiture. In his own lifetime he created an image of the court of Charles I which has since become the 'official' one – an image of elegant courtiers tinged with melancholy, posed gracefully in a mellow landscape. In the years after his death, Van Dyck's dazzling portrait-style left its mark on every English portrait artist and laid the foundation for the achievements of Gainsborough and Reynolds.

Van Dyck's early portraits, painted during his first Antwerp period, followed the conventional style of Dutch and Flemish portraiture. The sitters stand facing the spectator, posed stiffly against a plain dark background. But by around 1620, under the influence of the Venetian painters, and particularly that of Titian, Van Dyck had begun to create more complex settings for his subjects, placing them against a modest architectural background or a glimpse of landscape.

It was also from the Venetians that Van Dyck learnt how to break up the stiff frontality of the conventional Flemish portrait with a casual turn of the head, or a movement of the hand or foot.

These developments reached a peak in Van Dyck's magnificent Genoese portraits, which included his first full-lengths. Here, Van Dyck exploited the grandiose surroundings of his

François Langlois
(right) The sitter for this portrait was a dealer who secured works for Charles I and the Earl of Arundel. Van Dyck emphasises Langlois' talent for music, and his romantic but sympathetic and humorous disposition.

National Galleries of Scotland, Edinburgh

The Lomellini Family
(left) In this famous group portrait from his Genoese period, Van Dyck deliberately places the figures in a grandiose setting, so that even the children seem aware of their own dignity.

National Gallery of Art, Washington

An aristocratic patron
(above) Van Dyck's fine and detailed treatment of the Marchesa Elena Grimaldi contrasts sharply with the freely-painted figure of her servant, and adds visual interest to this portrait.

Fotomas

Cowdray Park, Sussex

Bridgeman Art Library

Private Collection

Rijksmuseum, Amsterdam

A royal union
(left) One of Van Dyck's most important commissions was to paint the young Prince William of Orange and Princess Mary Stuart, on their marriage in 1641.

A preparatory sketch
(above) A swift but tender sketch of Charles I's younger children – a preliminary to a group portrait – shows Van Dyck's sensitivity as a painter of infants.

patrons' palaces with exceptional skill. The architectural backgrounds of these portraits are used firstly to create a stable composition, as in *The Lomellini Family* (opposite), where the background of niches and columns forms a solid framework for the figures. Secondly, and most important, the architecture is used to emphasize the dignity and status of the sitters.

In the *Portrait of Elena Grimaldi* (opposite) for example, the fluted columns on the right are used to accentuate the slender proportions and upright stance of the *marchesa*, in marked contrast to the stooping attitude of her servant. Van Dyck further emphasizes the sitter's elevated position by adopting a low view-point so that the figure appears to tower over the spectator, and over the landscape beyond. Van Dyck's ablity to integrate his sitters with their backgrounds, and to create an environment which subtly flattered his subjects, constituted an important element in his success.

ITALIAN INFLUENCE

When Van Dyck arrived in England, portraiture at the English court was dominated by Dutch and Flemish portrait artists such as Daniel Mytens, who had been summoned to England by the Earl of Arundel. Van Dyck's dazzling Italianate style must have come as a revelation to his

Broadlands, Hants

TRADEMARKS

Graceful Hands

To indicate the artistocratic birth and bearing of his subjects, Van Dyck often depicted them with elegant – and elegantly drooping – wrists and hands.

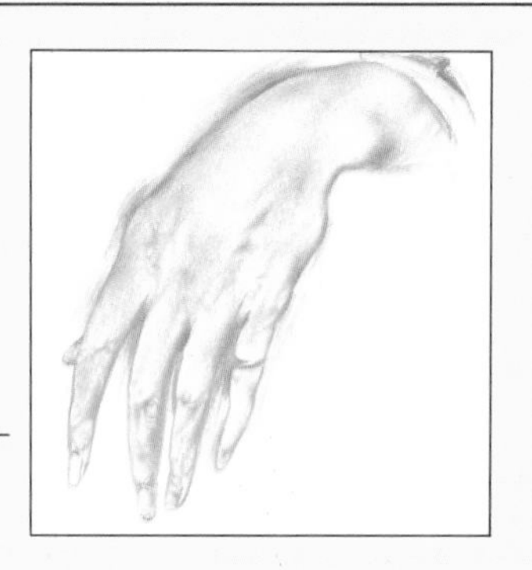

contemporaries and, shortly after his appointment as King's Painter, Mytens faded from the scene.

When in England, Van Dyck's portrait-style underwent a perceptible change. With a few notable exceptions such as *The Pembroke Family* group portrait, and the portraits of the King, the backgrounds of the English portraits are less sumptuous and more generalized, often being reduced to a single architectural 'prop' such as a column, broken up by a large piece of flowing drapery. Such changes probably reflect the fact that Van Dyck was working largely in his own studio, rather than in the homes of his sitters. At the same time Van Dyck began to focus more closely on the details and textures of his sitters' costumes, painting them with unequalled skill.

Unlike Rubens, Van Dyck approached his paintings in terms of surface and line. Consequently his figures occupy a relatively shallow space, which brings them close to the front of the painting. Their movements and gestures

Two brothers
(above left and detail) One of Van Dyck's most brilliant portraits depicts Lord John and Lord Bernard Stuart in the splendid attire and with the graceful hauteur that were the hallmarks of the cavalier. Both brothers died a few years later in the Civil War.

Character studies
(right) These wonderful sketches of a head, seen from different angles, show Van Dyck's interest in a popular 17th-century tradition.

run across the surface of the picture, creating elegant linear rhythms; they rarely move away from us into the distance, or turn at sharp angles to the picture plane. Rubens, on the other hand, was concerned with solid form. His passionate interest in sculpture led him to think of his painted figures as truly three-dimensional. Van Dyck's figures are less substantial and seem to be painted in webs of surface colour.

SUBTLE FLATTERY

Van Dyck's success as a portraitist depended partly on his ability to get the best out of his sitters. Although he retained a keen eye for the individual, he subtly flattered sitters by giving them slender, attenuated figures, elegant hands and graceful, dignified movements. Not surprisingly, his female portraits are the most idealized, although not all his female sitters were pleased with the results. The Countess of Sussex clearly thought that Van Dyck had not flattered her enough, and complained that the portrait '. . . makes me quite out of love with myself, the face is so big and so fat. . . it looks like one of the winds puffing.'

But, for the most part, Van Dyck's female sitters display less individuality than the Countess of Sussex and many show a striking resemblance to the image Van Dyck created of the Queen, Henrietta Maria. The Queen was certainly no beauty. The King's young niece, Princess Sophia, having become accustomed to Van Dyck's portraits, expressed her surprise on finding the Queen to be 'a little woman, with long lean arms, crooked shoulders, and teeth protruding from her mouth like guns from a fort.'

Van Dyck retained the ambition to be a successful history-painter, and was also sought after for his religious canvases. But his real achievement was in portraiture where, in the words of the critic De Piles, he combined 'Great Character of Spirit, Nobleness, Grace and Truth.'

Private Collection

COMPARISONS

Equestrian Portraits

The equestrian portrait originated in classical times. The prototype for all later versions was the bronze statue of the Roman Emperor Marcus Aurelius which stood on the Capitol in Rome. During the time of the Roman Empire, the equestrian portrait was reserved for the Emperor alone, so the model of the Marcus Aurelius carried associations of imperial power. In his two mounted portraits of Charles I, Van Dyck capitalized on these associations, consciously depicting Charles as the 'Emperor' of Great Britain. Van Dyck was also influenced by Rubens who painted numerous imposing versions of the equestrian portrait including *A Knight of the Golden Fleece*.

Sir Peter Paul Rubens (1577-1640) **A Knight of the Golden Fleece** *(right) Painted in about 1610, this portrait of a noble warrior and steed was emulated by Van Dyck, and strongly influenced European equestrian portraiture.*

Sir Edwin Landseer (1802-1873) **Queen Victoria at Osborne** *(below) Landseer approaches the equestrian theme with greater informality, showing the Queen seated on her horse reading a letter, her groom and dogs in attendance.*

Royal Collection

Royal Collection

THE MAKING OF A MASTERPIECE

Charles I in Three Positions

Van Dyck painted this magnificent portrait as a model for the Italian sculptor Bernini, who had been commissioned to make a marble bust of the King. The bust had been requested by the Queen, Henrietta Maria, and the commission was arranged by the sculptor's chief patron, Pope Urban VIII. The Pope's cooperation was largely a diplomatic gesture for he had hopes that Charles I would lead England back to the Catholic church.

The portrait was begun in the summer of 1635 and was sent to the sculptor in Rome the following year. The bust was despatched to England under special escort in April 1637, after it had been on public exhibition in Rome, and was presented to the King and Queen three months later. It was rapturously received, both for 'the exquisiteness of the work' and the 'likeness and near resemblance it had to the King's countenance'.

The commission was an important one for Van Dyck, since he knew that the portrait would be seen by the most important patrons and collectors in Rome. He clearly took particular pains with the work, giving it a degree of detail and refinement not strictly necessary for the sculptor's purposes but which might attract favourable attention from patrons. Bernini was reputedly struck by the King's air of brooding melancholy, ironically remarking that his countenance seemed to forebode unhappiness.

'No king . . . has been imaged in such variety of genius.'

Sir David Piper

Subtle colouring
(below) The colour scheme of the portrait is of great beauty, especially in the contrast between the three different costumes worn by the King.

Characteristic features
(right) Van Dyck modelled Charles I's head with extreme care and delicacy, capturing to perfection his heavy-lidded eyes, long nose and fine hair.

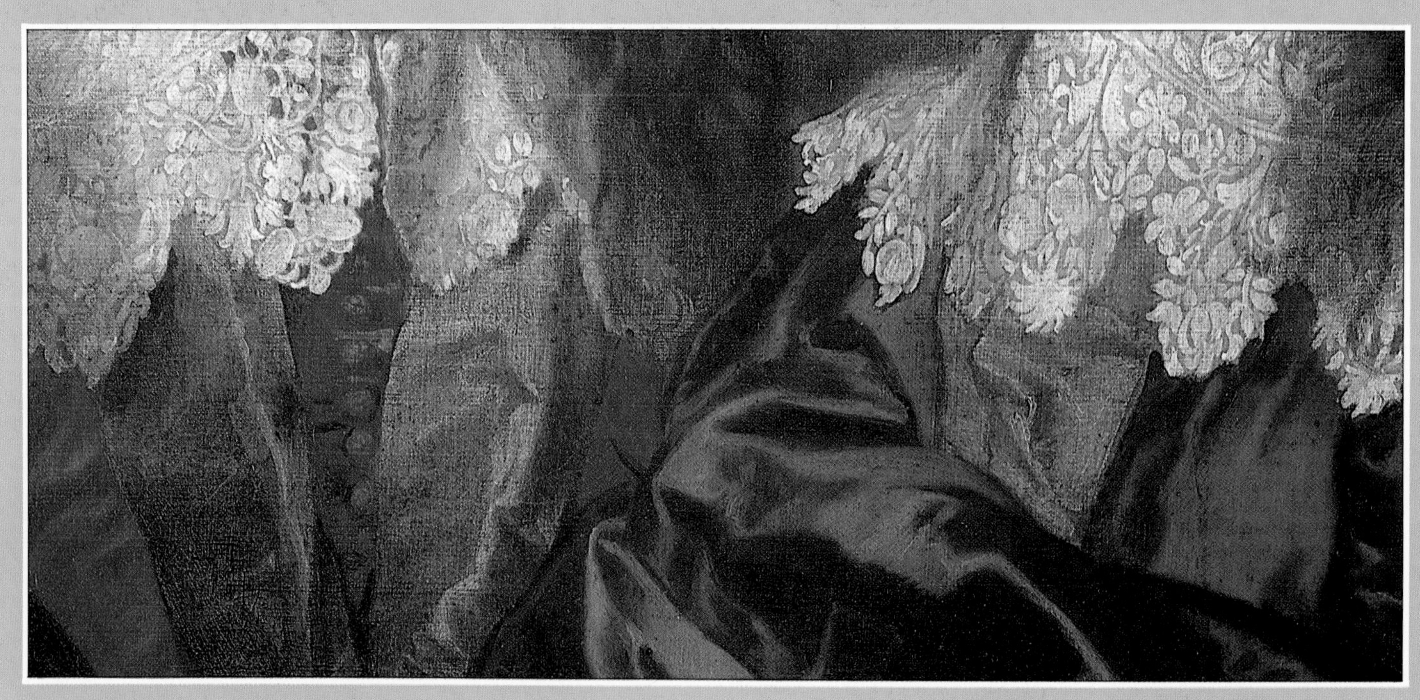

After Bernini
(above) The original Bernini bust was lost in a fire at Whitehall Palace in 1698, and a copy was subsequently made, perhaps from a cast. All the familiar details are present, including the characteristically uneven hair length.

A further commission
(below) Van Dyck painted three portraits of Queen Henrietta Maria, in profile and full-face, for a bust of herself which she commissioned from Bernini in 1639. But the portraits were never sent because of England's increasing civil turmoil.

Kunsthistorisches Museum, Vienna

Van Dyck's inspiration
(above) Lorenzo Lotto's famous triple portrait of a jeweller hung at Whitehall in Van Dyck's time – with an attribution to Titian – and very likely provided part of the inspiration for Van Dyck's own work.

Reproduced by gracious permission of Her Majesty the Queen/Royal Collection

Gallery

Van Dyck is celebrated as one of the greatest of all portraitists. The splendour of his compositions, the elegant ease with which he invested his sitters and his brilliant skills in painting fine materials made him the ideal court artist, and his portraits of Charles I, his wife Henrietta Maria and the royal children have given to their era a unique romantic aura.

Scala

Christ Crowned with Thorns *c.1620*
88″ × 77″ Prado, Madrid

Van Dyck painted two closely similar versions of this picture at about the same time; the other one was in Berlin, but was destroyed during the Second World War. No doubt a patron was impressed by the work and commissioned a replica. The heavy musculature of the figures shows the overwhelming influence of Rubens on the young Van Dyck.

Although Van Dyck was so often concerned with creating a public image, he responded with great sensitivity to individual character, as his portraits of Philippe le Roy and his wife Marie de Raet clearly show.

Van Dyck's genius extended beyond portraiture however. Especially in his early career, he painted some memorable religious works, notably The Rest on the Flight into Egypt, with its personal vein of melancholy. And the sensuous beauty of Cupid and Psyche, thought to be the only mythological work Van Dyck did in England, makes it regrettable that the demand for portraits left him little time for more such works.

Joachim Blauel/Artothek

The Rest on the Flight into Egypt *c.1630*
52¾" × 42½" Alte Pinakothek, Munich

This is one of Van Dyck's tenderest religious paintings and one of the masterpieces of his second Antwerp period (1628-32) between his lengthy stays in Italy and England. Van Dyck was remarkably sensitive to female beauty, and the head of the Virgin, with its poignant, troubled expression, is one of the loveliest he ever painted.

Philippe le Roy, Seigneur de Ravels
1630
84½" × 48½"
Wallace Collection, London

This and the picture opposite are among the most magnificent portraits of Van Dyck's second Antwerp period. Philippe le Roy, who was 34 when the portrait was painted, was counsellor to the Archduke Ferdinand, Governor of the Netherlands. The imposing sense of height and elegance with which Van Dyck invests the sitter is emphasized by the sleek greyhound, an appropriate choice of dog for such a graceful man.

Marie de Raet
1631
84¼″ × 48½″
Wallace Collection,
London

Marie de Raet married Philippe le Roy (opposite) in 1631, when she was 16, and this picture – with a matching background – was painted to mark the occasion. Van Dyck clearly differentiates between the characters of the husband and wife; whereas Philippe is a man of the world, Marie looks rather shy and unsure of herself, as well she might at such a tender age. In place of the sporting animal of her husband, she has a tiny lapdog.

Charles I on Horseback with Seigneur de St Antoine *1633*
145″ × 106″ Royal Collection

This breathtakingly impressive equestrian portrait was originally hung at the end of the Long Gallery in Whitehall Palace and from a distance must have produced the effect that the King was riding in triumph through the painted arch into the building. Seigneur de St Antoine was Charles' riding master and equerry.

Queen Henrietta Maria with her Dwarf Sir Jeffrey Hudson *1633*
86½″ × 53″ National Gallery of Art, Washington

Dwarfs were commonly kept for amusement in the courts of 17th-century Europe. Hudson (1619-82) came to the attention of the King and Queen when he emerged from a pie at a dinner given in their honour by the Duchess of Buckingham, in whose service he then was. At that time he was said to be about 18 inches tall, but he grew to about 4 feet.

Charles I in Three Positions *1635*
33¼″ × 39¼″ Royal Collection

Van Dyck painted this portrait to send to Rome to enable Gianlorenzo Bernini, the greatest sculptor of the day, to carve a marble bust of the King. By a curious coincidence, the great French painter Philippe de Champaigne painted a similar triple portrait of Cardinal Richelieu at about the same time (see p. 104), and this, too, was sent to Rome to have a bust carved from it; the identity of the sculptor is uncertain. Van Dyck's portrait remained in the possession of Bernini's descendants until 1802, but it returned to the royal collection in 1822 when it was bought by George IV at Christie's for 1000 guineas.

Reproduced by gracious permission of Her Majesty the Queen

Five Children of Charles I *1637*
64½″ × 78¼″ Royal Collection

This is the latest and most ambitious of Van Dyck's portraits of the royal children and he took great pains over its planning, making preparatory drawings of individual figures and a beautiful oil study of the two youngest children (p.83) on the right of this painting. Each child is characterized with great delicacy and the quality of the brushwork is superlative. The animal and still life details, as well as the children, are brilliantly depicted.

Cupid and Psyche *c.1638*
78½" × 76¾" Royal Collection

This poetic and beautifully coloured painting – the only mythological work that Van Dyck is known to have done in England – was painted for Charles I. The involved story of Cupid (the god of Love) and Psyche (the personification of the human soul) was interpreted as an allegory of the search of the Soul for union with Desire.

Lady Elizabeth Thimbleby and Dorothy, Viscountess Andover *c.1637*
52″ × 59″ National Gallery, London

The sitters were sisters, daughters of Thomas, Viscount Savage. As Lady Andover, on the right, is receiving roses from a Cupid, it is thought likely that the painting was commissioned to celebrate her wedding in April 1637.

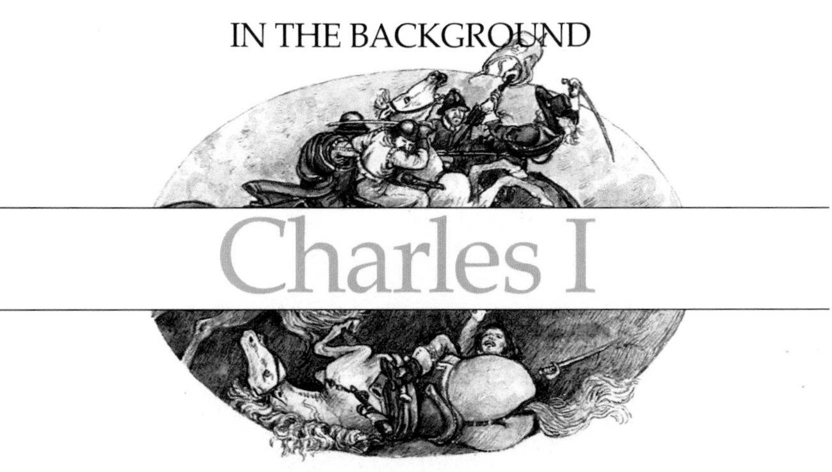

Charles I

Life at the court of Charles I was luxurious and cultured. But the King's military ventures and mishandling of Parliament made him increasingly unpopular and led to civil war and his own execution.

When Anthony Van Dyck arrived in England in 1632 to serve at the court of Charles I, Charles was just entering the happiest period of his life. The bitter strife of the early years of his reign was over, and the terrible civil wars that would ravage the country were still a decade away. His newly discovered affection for his young French wife was blossoming and the two children she had borne him – Charles in 1630 and Mary in 1631 – enriched the family atmosphere at Whitehall. Over the next few years, Charles's court was to become one of the most cultured and fashionable in Europe.

The memory of the Duke of Buckingham's assassination four years before, however, was still acutely painful and infused his rather reserved air with the touch of melancholy that Van Dyck was to capture superbly in his portraits. Buckingham, the beautiful young man Charles' father James I had doted on so unashamedly, had been his mentor and dearest friend, and the Duke's death affected him deeply.

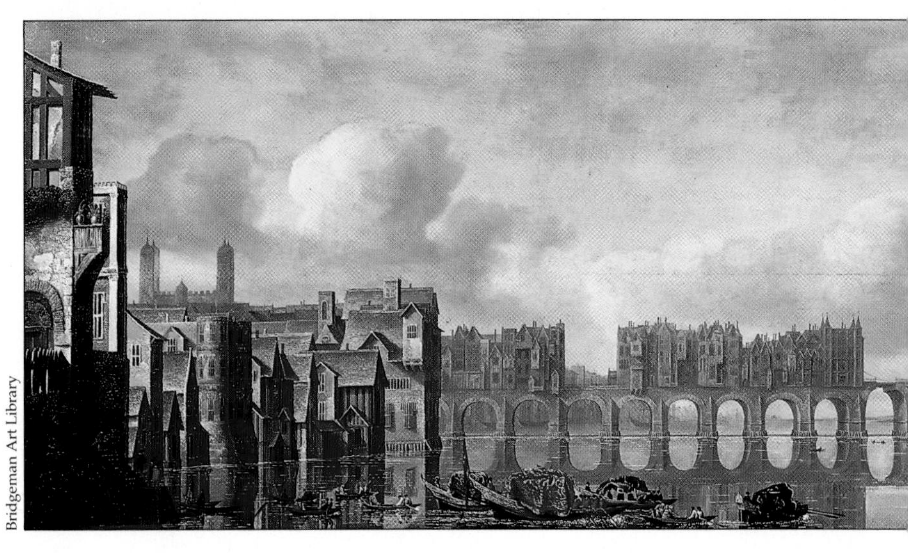

Bridgeman Art Library

Contemporary London *(above) 17th-century London was a thriving city whose wealth derived from its busy port. This painting shows the old London Bridge, which was less than a mile downstream from Blackfriars, where Charles I used to visit Van Dyck in his studio.*

Bridgeman Art Library

Robert Peake; Charles I when Duke of York/City of Bristol Museum and Art Gallery

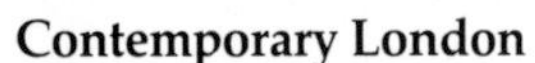

The young Charles *(left) Born in 1600, the second son of James I, young Charles was a feeble child who suffered from a stutter. He became heir to the throne in 1612 when his elder and more accomplished brother Henry died of a fever, and was finally proclaimed King of England in 1625.*

Nine years earlier, while James was still King, the two friends had set off on a reckless romantic adventure, donning false beards to ride virtually alone right across France and on to Madrid to woo the King of Spain's daughter. The quest had come to nothing, but Buckingham returned with his heart set on an aggressive foreign policy – which Charles backed to the hilt. Over the next six years, they had mounted a series of military ventures against the continental powers Spain and France, all of which ended in embarassing failure – that to Cadiz because the English troops' first discovery on landing was a wine store, that to the French Isle of Ré because the scaling ladders fell just short of the top of the town walls, and that to La Rochelle because the intrepid Lord Denbigh was unnerved by a chain strung across the estuary.

THE ABUSE OF PARLIAMENT

While James I was still alive, Charles and Buckingham had often exploited Parliament unashamedly to force the King's hand and silence opposition. And after Charles became King in

1625, he called Parliament three times – in 1625, 1626 and 1628 – mainly to vote money to fund Buckingham's military ventures. With each successive failure, however, MPs resented being used in this way more and more – no doubt encouraged by the assault on their purses – and began to voice their objections ever more stridently.

In each of Charles' first three Parliaments, Buckingham was attacked fiercely and the King could only forestall the attacks by dissolving Parliament. Then in 1628, Buckingham was assassinated. When the whole country seemed to celebrate his death, Charles was deeply hurt. Another snub in Parliament in early 1629 seemed the last straw and he resolved to do without it. In March that year, he dissolved Parliament, seemingly forever, and arrested those men he believed to be the culprits. Within two years, he had concluded peace treaties with France and Spain, abandoning the aggressive policy that needed parliamentary support, and retreated to the private world of his court. For the next nine years he virtually retired from politics, leaving the day-to-day running of the country to ministers and casting only cursory glances over state papers.

The one consolation for Charles from Buckingham's death was that he fell in love with

Mary Evans Picture Library

A sumptuous court
(above) The court of Charles I was one of the most magnificent and cultured in Europe, attracting writers, artists and musicians from England and abroad. It made a stark contrast with the miserable life of the masses.

Claude De Jongh; London Bridge in the 16th Century/Kenwood House, London

Detail: Peter Lely; Sovereign of the Seas

National Maritime Museum, Greenwich

The King's flagship
(right) In order to pursue his independent foreign policy, Charles spent vast sums of money building up his navy. His flagship was Sovereign of the Seas. Launched in 1637, it was the most powerful ship of its time, and was one of many funded by the despised 'Ship Money' which Charles levied from the port and inland counties.

Reproduced by gracious permission of Her Majesty the Queen

Royal Collection

A Catholic Queen
(left) Van Dyck's painting of Henrietta Maria is an idealized portrait of the Queen in her early 30s. The youngest daughter of Henry IV of France, she married Charles soon after his coronation in 1625 when she was just 15. Although she had little influence on English politics, she was perceived as a Catholic threat by the population at large.

his wife for the first time. He had married Henrietta Maria, the 15-year-old daughter of the French King Henry IV, in 1625 when the Spanish match fell through, but their first night ended in tears. Within six weeks they were living apart.

A TEMPESTUOUS MARRIAGE

Henrietta Maria had been brought up to believe it was her duty to convert the English back to Catholicism, and to her missionary zeal she added a fiery temper and a scowl that would send men scurrying. The first four years of her marriage to Charles were invariably stormy and their frequent arguments sent her charging round Whitehall Palace smashing windows. Their differences were ostensibly religious but often their quarrels could be far from high-minded – the French ambassador was once called in to settle a dispute over whether it was raining or not. Buckingham's death, however, seemed to ease the tension between them and the birth of their first child, Charles, in May 1630, set the seal on their reconciliation.

Despite the fact that they had nine children, Charles' and Henrietta Maria's love seems to have been affectionate rather than passionate and their relationship set the tone for the whole court. Their court became a model of decorum and gracious living, and the concept of courtly love allowed the young French queen to be surrounded by young, fashionably-dressed and handsome men without a whiff of scandal. Charles' love of the arts also brought many poets, artists and musicians to the court to celebrate the virtues of romance.

Bridgeman Art Library

Ernest Crofts; Cromwell After the Battle of Marston Moor/Burnley Art Gallery

In the first 15 years of Charles' reign, over 400 plays and masques were staged at the court by playwrights such as Beaumont and Fletcher and Ben Jonson, and the young court poets such as Richard Lovelace, Thomas Carew and Robert Herrick established their own style of romantic 'cavalier' poetry. As a patron of art, Charles is unrivalled by any English monarch: he not only commissioned paintings by Rubens and Van Dyck and sculptures by Bernini but built a vast and carefully-chosen collection of some of the greatest masterpieces of European art. But while the court played and Charles indulged in his favourite past-times – art collection, hunting and supervising the rebuilding of the Royal Navy – all was far from well in England.

Beyond the court, times were exceptionally hard, with the disruption of the vital cloth trade by the Thirty Years War on the continent, poor harvest and some of the coldest winters ever known. More ominous, perhaps, was the growing resentment to the policy of 'fiscal feudalism' used by Crown Agents to obtain money in the absence

Mansell Collection

The King's last stand

(left) Following Charles' military defeat in the Civil War, the army forced Parliament to bring the King to trial in January 1649. He was found guilty of treason and publicly executed.

Lauros-Giraudon

of Parliament – particularly annoying were impositions such as the 'knighthood fines' by which anyone worth £40 a year who had not attended Charles' coronation to be knighted was fined heavily.

To these material grievances was added growing opposition to the 'popish' influence of Charles' French queen and to the Church reforms being pushed through by Archbishop Laud. Although Laud denied vigorously, and sincerely, that he was a Catholic, his reforms seemed to be imposing the same kind of rigid clerical hierarchy on the English Church that had provoked the Protestant Reformation a century before.

Throughout the 1630s, these tensions were gradually building up and then, towards the end of the decade, they exploded. Laud's attempt, with Charles' backing, to force a new prayer book on the Scottish church in 1637 ended with the Scots forming a covenant in opposition. Two wars failed to subdue the Scots, and to fund the war effort Charles was forced to recall Parliament in April 1640 and again in November. By the time Van Dyck died the following year, Parliament had become the focus for opposition and the country was well down the road to the civil wars that were to end in defeat for the royalists and the execution of Charles in January 1649.

The Civil War
(left) In 1642 England drifted into civil war. The King's first major defeat at the hands of Cromwell's army was at the battle of Marston Moor, in July 1644.

Loyal Cavaliers
(below) Charles Louis and Rupert were nephews of Charles I. During the Civil War Rupert distinguished himself fighting for the King.

Mansell Collection

The Eikon Basilike
(above) During his captivity Charles helped to write The Eikon Basilike *– a pamphlet portraying him as a Christian king who was martyred for his faith. Designed to undermine the Commonwealth, it became immensely popular after Charles' execution.*

The rule of Cromwell
(right) After the King's death Cromwell ruled with an iron fist, clashing violently with Parliament, which he dissolved in 1658 – the year of his death. Eighteen months later Charles II was restored to the throne.

Fotomas

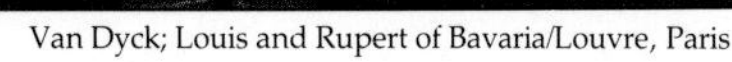
Van Dyck; Louis and Rupert of Bavaria/Louvre, Paris

National Portrait Gallery

A Year in the Life 1635

By 1635 Van Dyck had become a familiar figure at the English court. England at this time was both peaceful and prosperous, in marked contrast to Europe where the war had entered its seventeenth year and France was at last openly challenging the supremacy of Spain.

In 1635, after six years of personal rule (which his enemies were eventually to label 'the Eleven Years Tyranny'), Charles I was faced with little concerted opposition from his British subjects. However, government without parliament also meant doing without the taxes that only parliament could authorize.

During the previous year the King had successfully raised Ship Money from the coastal areas. This levy, made from time to time during the Middle Ages, was to finance new ships for the navy which seemed reasonable enough since the fleet was badly run down and England was troubled by the depredations of Barbary pirates. However, in 1635 Charles broke with tradition by extending the levy to the inland counties, arguing that there was little reason why the maritime ports should bear the whole charge.

Mauro Pucciarelli

Bibliothèque Nationale, Paris

Michael Friedel/Image Bank

Creator of French classical tragedy
(above) Pierre Corneille, whose abilities as a comic playwright had attracted the notice and later the patronage of Richelieu, turned to writing tragedy in 1635 with his play Médée.

French occupy Martinique
(above right) The French Compagnie des Isles d'Amérique formally took possession of the Caribbean island of Martinique in June 1635, later to be the birthplace of Josephine Bonaparte.

Philippe de Champaigne/Triple Portrait of the Head of Richelieu/National Gallery, London

The many faces of Cardinal Richelieu
(right) The French minister was much occupied in 1635. He renewed an alliance with Sweden, organized a league against Milan and ensured the official recognition of the Académie Française.

Most people paid up but the following year a Buckinghamshire landowner named John Hampden refused on principle to hand over a small sum (twenty shillings) and his case eventually became a focus for opposition to royal policy. The apparent tranquillity of English society was disturbed, though civil war and the overthrow of the monarchy still lay some years away.

FRANCO-SPANISH POWER STRUGGLE

On the continent, the Thirty Years War (1618-48) was entering a new phase. This had so far been a war in which Catholics fought Protestants. The main protagonists on the Catholic side were the Spanish and Austrian Habsburgs (the latter including the Holy Roman Emperors), whose enemies included the Dutch and the Protestant princes of the Empire, aided first by the Danes and later by the Swedes. The Protestants received covert help – in the way of generous subsidies from France. Although predominantly Catholic with the chief minister, Cardinal Richelieu, a prince of the Church, France had every interest in weakening the Habsburgs and replacing them as the dominant force in Europe.

In September 1634 the apparently invincible Swedes suffered a crushing defeat at Nördlingen. As a result, the most important German Protestant princes signed a peace settlement with the Emperor at Prague in May 1635. A compromise was reached with regard to religion, which from this time onwards played only a minor part in the war. The Swedes, now

Ship money
(below) This tract, published in 1647 when the English King Charles I was a prisoner in Carisbrooke Castle on the Isle of Wight, harks back to the issue of Ship Money, raised 13 years earlier. The King, who had ruled without Parliament since 1629, was forced to revive this ancient levy in 1634 to rebuild the navy, extending it the next year to the inland counties. The furore excited by subsequent demands led inexorably to the outbreak of civil war.

The Archangel Michael
(right) This powerful work by the Bolognese artist, Guido Reni (1575-1642), who is generally acknowledged as one of the finest of Italian Baroque painters, was commissioned by Cardinal San'Onofrio, brother of Pope Urban VIII, and executed in about 1635. The painting was highly celebrated in the literature of the time as an image of 'Ideal Beauty', the colouring and the pose of the Archangel being typical of Reni's style.

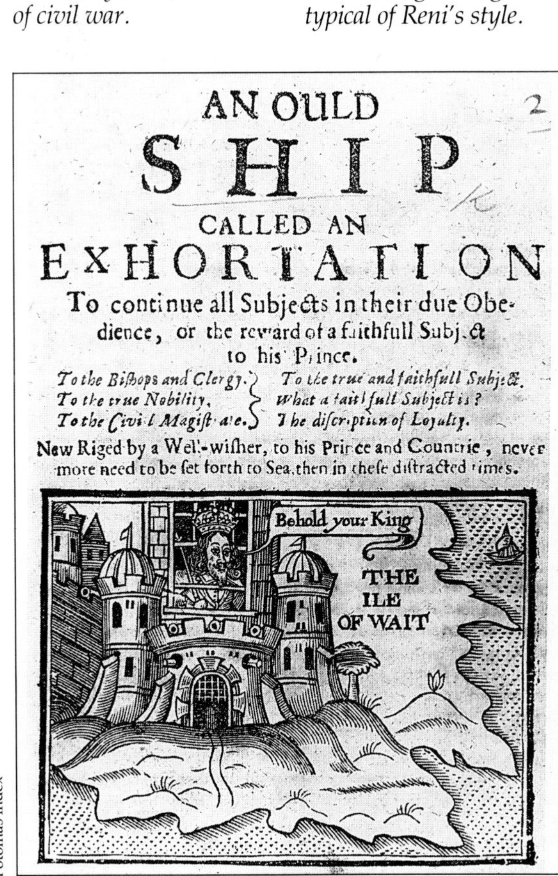

AN OULD
SHIP
CALLED AN
EXHORTATION
To continue all Subjects in their due Obedience, or the reward of a faithfull Subject to his Prince.

To the Bishops and Clergy. To the true Nobility, To the Civil Magistrate. — To the true and faithfull Subject. What a faithfull Subject is? The discription of Loyalty.

New Riged by a Well-wisher, to his Prince and Countrie, never more need to be set forth to Sea, then in these distracted times.

Fotomas Index

Guido Reni/The Archangel Michael/Capuchin Church, Rome

dangerously isolated, told Richelieu bluntly that they could only carry on if France entered the struggle on their side and although the Cardinal's preparations were far from complete, he was forced to agree. In May 1635, with curiously outmoded ceremony, a French herald and trumpeter entered the Grande Place in Brussels (capital of the Spanish Netherlands), proclaimed their master's grievance, and flung a declaration of war into the assembled crowd.

Richelieu's diplomacy and French money quickly created a motley coalition including the Swedes, the Dutch, the able mercenary general, Bernard of Saxe-Weimar, and the rulers of Parma and Savoy. For the first year, the inexperienced French army achieved little. The only exception was a curious one. There was a Protestant revolt in the Valtelline, the Alpine pass through which Spanish and Habsburg troops could march into central Europe. Characteristically, the Cardinal dispatched a French Protestant force, under the Huguenot Duc de Rohan, to 'liberate' their co-religionists. For the time being, at least, this vital link had fallen into French hands.

Richelieu's other notable action in 1635 lay in a quite different field. He set up the Académie Française on a formal basis and entrusted it with the task of maintaining the purity of literary French and preparing an authoritative dictionary. This famous institution is still restricted to forty members, whom Diderot irreverently referred to as 'forty geese that guard the Capitol', since they have generally been ultra-conservative in outlook. Nevertheless, to most Frenchmen today, they remain 'the immortals'.

Antwerp's Baroque welcome
(right) This Stage of Welcome was part of the pageantry devised for the formal entry of the Cardinal-Infante Ferdinand, the new Governor-General of the Netherlands, into Antwerp in April 1635. The right-hand panel depicts the Infante, younger brother of Philip IV of Spain, shaking hands with his cousin, the King of Hungary, before their combined forces crushed the Swedes at the Battle of Nördlingen the previous September. The whole spectacle, which included several triumphal arches, was designed by Peter Paul Rubens.

Fotomas Index

A Venetian landmark
(below) The Church of Santa Maria della Salute is the supreme masterpiece of Venetian Baroque architecture and of its architect, Baldassare Longhena (1598-1682), the name 'Salute' signifying 'health' as the church was dedicated to the Virgin Mary as a thanksgiving for the ending of a virulent plague which swept through Venice in 1630. Although construction was under way by 1635, it was not completed until 1687. The church is now a familiar sight, its famous silhouette dominating the entrance to the Grand Canal.

Jörg P. Anders

Canaletto/S Maria della Salute, Venice/Staatliche Museen Preussischer Kulturbesitz, Berlin (West)

1628/9-1682

Jacob van Ruisdael was the outstanding landscape painter of the late seventeenth century. He was born into a family of painters working in Haarlem, which included his uncle Salomon van Ruysdael, one of the most talented landscapists of the previous generation. Salomon almost certainly trained Ruisdael, but the boy soon abandoned his uncle's quiet, restrained style in favour of a more dramatic and exuberant approach.

Ruisdael spent most of his career in Amsterdam where he found a secure market for his landscapes, and particularly for his exotic views of mountain scenery. The details of his life remain obscure but he seems to have been a pious and melancholy man with a poet's talent for infusing his works with atmosphere and mood. He may also have practised as a surgeon in Amsterdam, although this remains unconfirmed.

Dutch Landscape Master

Ruisdael was born in Haarlem, but moved to Amsterdam as his landscape paintings found greater favour. Intriguingly, it seems that he may even have found time to practise as a surgeon in the city.

Jacob van Ruisdael was born in Haarlem in about 1628 or 1629, the son of Isaack van Ruisdael, and his second wife, Maycken Cornelisdr. There is no record of his birth, but in 1661 he declared in a legal document that he was 32. The boy's early circumstances must certainly have influenced his decision to become a painter. He came, firstly, from an artistic family. His father, although chiefly a frame-maker and art dealer by trade, was also a minor painter and is known to have designed cartoons for tapestries. He painted a few landscapes, but none of these survives. More important, Jacob's uncle, Salomon van Ruysdael (the difference in spelling occurs in their signatures), was one of the most talented landscape painters of the early 17th century and a respected member of the Haarlem Guild of St Luke. Jacob remained close to his uncle throughout his life, and Salomon presumably gave him much of his early instruction.

The city of Haarlem was, furthermore, the home of the Dutch school of landscape painting. Before the beginning of the 17th century, there had been little landscape painting as such in the Northern Provinces (the modern-day Netherlands). Only a few artists had painted independent landscapes, and they were mainly immigrants from Flanders. In the two decades before Jacob's birth, however, an outstanding generation of painters had developed a specifically Dutch type of landscape painting, a genre which became instantly successful. Jacob's uncle was one of the foremost members of this group of painters, together with the masters Esaias van de Velde and Jan van Goyen.

ARTISTIC CONNECTIONS

These three artists lived or worked in Haarlem at some time in their careers. So as a child, Jacob came into contact with some of the most influential painters of the day. His father seems to have had particularly close connections with Jan van Goyen, for in 1634 the latter was fined three guilders by the Haarlem Guild for painting pictures in Isaack's house. Although he was staying in Haarlem, van Goyen was not a member of the Guild, and was thus prohibited from working in the town.

Majestic ruins
(above) Throughout his life, Ruisdael travelled in search of fresh artistic inspiration, although he never strayed far from home. In the 1650s he made an excursion to the castle of Egmond, near Alkmaar, and the ruined site made a profound impression on him. He sketched and painted the castle (see pp.112-13) from several different views.

Key Dates

1628/29 born in Haarlem

c.1646 joins Haarlem Guild of St Luke

1646 produces first signed and dated work

1650s travels to the Dutch/German border with Nicolaes Berchem

c.1656 moves to Amsterdam

1657 becomes baptized into the Reformed Church

1667 makes his will

c.1670 moves to Sweerts' shop near the Dam

1681 death of Jacob Salomonsz. van Ruysdael

1682 Ruisdael dies in Amsterdam and is buried in Haarlem

Klaus Kerth/Zefa

Native town
(above) Ruisdael was born in Haarlem in 1628 or 1629. The city was a thriving artistic and industrial centre, and had become exceptionally prosperous through its linen-bleaching trade. Its success was a source of great civic pride.

Early influence
(right) Ruisdael's career was considerably influenced by the lyrical landscapes of another Haarlem artist, Cornelis Vroom. Vroom was described in a local history as the finest painter of 'our fields, woods and forests'.

Ruins of the Castle Egmond, Rijksmuseum, Amsterdam

there are a few scattered indications that he may also have practised as a doctor of medicine. In his biography of Ruisdael, published in 1721, the painter and writer Arnold Houbraken claimed that Ruisdael had begun to study medicine at an early age, and that he 'performed several surgical operations in Amsterdam and gained a wide reputation'. These suggestions are difficult to reconcile with Ruisdael's large output as a painter (about 700 pictures are attributed to him), and it has been often assumed that Houbraken confused him with another doctor of the same name. Nonetheless, other odd facts seem to support Houbraken's claim.

In 1720, for example (the year before Houbraken's biography was published), the compiler of a sale catalogue for an auction in Dordrecht listed a painting as 'a very ingenious

The Castle at Bentheim
(below) In the early 1650s, Ruisdael visited the border region. The hilly, wooded landscape must have made an exciting change from the flat countryside around Haarlem.

Work for a wealthy patron
(bottom) Ruisdael collaborated with the painter Thomas de Keyser on this conversation piece for the rich and powerful burgomaster, Cornelis de Graeff.

Few details are known of Ruisdael's life, and the circumstances of his early training remain obscure. It seems likely that he trained initially with his uncle, although their styles remained highly distinct. Ruisdael was certainly exceptionally precocious; his earliest dated works are of 1646, when he was at most 18, but they show no trace of immaturity. By this time he must have been a member of the Guild, since this was a condition of working independently in the city. He would have been unusually young for Guild membership, but he may have been given a concession on account of his obviously outstanding artistic talent.

Our hazy knowledge of Ruisdael's life is especially tantalizing in one particular respect, for

The Alfred Beit Foundation

Landscape with a River by a Wood, National Gallery, London

The Arrival of Cornelis de Graeff at Soestdijk, National Gallery of Ireland

A Talented Family

Ruisdael's father, Isaack, was a painter and tapestry designer, and had connections with some of the most influential of the Haarlem landscapists – in 1634, Jan van Goyen was fined 3 guilders for painting pictures in Isaack's house, against guild regulations. More important, Ruisdael's uncle Salomon was one of the most talented members of the first generation of Dutch landscape artists, and a prominent member of the Haarlem guild. Salomon almost certainly trained Ruisdael, although his influence on his nephew's style is difficult to detect. Salomon's son, Jacob Salomonszson (usually shortened to Salomonsz.) also became a painter, although he was notably less gifted than his father. He went insane and died in great poverty in an Almshouse.

National Gallery, London

Mauritshuis, The Hague

Landscape with Waterfall by a Cottage
(above) Like Ruisdael, Jacob Salomonsz. was influenced by the Scandinavian landscapes of Allart van Everdingen. Although technically accomplished, his variations on the Scandinavian theme are less inventive than Ruisdael's.

River Landscape
Salomon van Ruysdael's calm landscapes are typical of the Haarlem school of the early 17th century, and markedly different from Ruisdael's florid, exuberant style.

landscape with a waterfall, by Doctor Jacob Ruisdael'. And, the name 'Jacobus Ruijsdael' appears in an Amsterdam list of doctors, stating that he had received a medical degree at the University of Caen in north-western France in 1676 (at this time he was in his late 40s). In some ways this document serves to deepen the mystery, for, apart from there being no other evidence that Ruisdael ever went to Caen, the name on the list has been inexplicably crossed out. The truth of the matter will probably never be known.

During his early years in Haarlem, Ruisdael travelled quite extensively, although he never went far afield. He clearly had a liking for picturesque spots, and visited the picturesque ruined church at Egmond van Zee, and the Portuguese Jewish cemetery at Ouderkerk (p.122). During the 1650s he became more adventurous and explored the border region between the eastern provinces of the Netherlands and West Germany, travelling with his friend and collaborator Nicolaes Berchem, who sometimes painted the figures in Ruisdael's pictures.

Ruisdael stayed in Haarlem until around 1656, devoting himself to his career and his family.

Move to Amsterdam
(right) In c.1656 Ruisdael moved to Amsterdam where he was to remain until his death.

A practising doctor?
(below) The appearance – and mysterious crossing-out – of Ruisdael's name in the 'List of Amsterdam Doctors', adds a curious new dimension to his character.

Joseph F. Viesti/Susan Griggs

National Gallery, London

Pupil and companion *(above) Meindert Hobbema was Ruisdael's closest friend and his most gifted pupil. Hobbema's most famous work,* The Avenue at Middelharnis, *shows his preference for sunny, rather prosaic scenes. But the artist's wonderful gift of composition makes this one of the most memorable landscape paintings of all time.*

Gemeentearchief, Amsterdam

Although he was by no means rich, he seems to have provided financial support for his father (who constantly had money problems) from his earliest years.

In about 1656 Ruisdael moved to Amsterdam, where he was to stay for the rest of his life. A document of the 14 June 1657 in the records of Amsterdam's Reformed Church announces Ruisdael's intention to be baptized (it is not known what his religious affiliation was before he joined the Reformed Church). The ceremony took place one week later in the village of Ankerveen. Initially he settled in a house known as the 'Silvere Trompet', near the Dam, the city's main square. Ten years later, Ruisdael's cousin, Jacob Salomonsz., also moved to Amsterdam.

Like most Dutch painters of the period Ruisdael must have worked largely for the open market. Consequently, we have little information about his patrons. His only identified patron is the wealthy Amsterdam town-councillor Cornelis de Graeff, Lord of Zuidpolsbroek. In collaboration with the portraitist Thomas de Keyser, Ruisdael painted a picture of de Graeff and his family arriving at their country estate at Soestdijk (p.109).

In May 1667 Ruisdael made two wills. The wills described him as 'a bachelor, sick in body, but in possession of his physical and mental faculties'. In fact, Ruisdael lived for another 15 years, years which saw the production of some of his most original and inspired works. Around 1670, he took rooms on the south side of the Dam, above a shop kept by Hieronymous Sweerts, a book and art dealer. The two men clearly enjoyed a good relationship, and Sweerts published a number of Ruisdael's etchings.

DEATH OF A NAMESAKE

In 1681 Ruisdael's cousin went insane. He was taken to the Almshouse in Haarlem, where he died towards the end of the year. For many years a confusion between the two men (who were almost exact contemporaries as well as near namesakes) led to the belief that Ruisdael himself died in penury. In fact he earned good prices for his works up to the end of his life. Ruisdael himself died in Amsterdam, around 10 March 1682. His body was taken to Haarlem and buried in St Bavo's, a magnificent Gothic church.

THE ARTIST AT WORK

The Lyrical Painter

Ruisdael broke away from conventional Dutch landscape painting by choosing different subjects and by creating a sense of atmosphere, varying from the dramatic to brooding stillness.

National Gallery, London

A Pool Surrounded by Trees (c.1660s)
(above) Nature is seen to be dominant over man, impervious to his activities. The huntsmen coursing a hare are hardly visible among the towering trees – but intimations of the animal's mortality can be found in the stripped branches of the dead silver birches, illuminated by a brilliant shaft of light.

Landscape with the Ruins of the Castle of Egmond (early 1650s)
(right) Ruisdael's concern at the time of this painting was with elongated forms and solid masses. In depicting a ruin, he may have been making a comment on the durability of man's work – he was certainly not interested in accurate representation – the hill is imaginary.

In 1807, the French artist and critic Jean-Joseph Taillasson wrote of Ruisdael: 'One cannot find in the paintings of other artists of his country a poetry as moving as that which he puts into his own.' Goethe recognized the same lyrical quality in Ruisdael's work and wrote an essay entitled 'Ruisdael as Poet', stimulated in part by the enigmatic *Jewish Cemetery* (p.122). It is largely this poetic quality of Ruisdael's landscapes that makes them so distinct and memorable. His landscapes are never simply depictions of a particular site, whether real or imagined. In each of his works Ruisdael creates a mood, capturing the atmosphere evoked by a landscape under certain conditions of weather and light.

These qualities are most evident in the dramatic canvases of Ruisdael's later years, such as the *Extensive Landscape with a Ruined Castle* (p.129), or the mysterious *Coup de Soleil* (p.131). But an intensely lyrical feeling also pervades his more intimate works, such as the *Sunlit Grain Field on the Banks of a Coast* (p.125), or the *Winter Landscape* (p.128), which captures perfectly the silent, brooding air of a dark winter evening.

In the generation before Ruisdael, Dutch artists had concentrated on the accurate depiction of the lands around them. Inspired in part by the sense of national pride which developed in the new republic, artists such as Esaias van de Velde and Jan van Goyen focused their attention on the distinctive features of their native landscape. While their landscapes are not necessarily depictions of specific sites and were rarely painted outdoors, they aimed to recreate faithfully the typical characteristics of the Dutch countryside.

Because of this, their landscapes are essentially quiet and undramatic, for the landscape of the Netherlands is open and flat, and lacking in striking or picturesque views. The artist who attempted an extensive view was faced with a long expanse of flat polderland, unbroken by dramatic 'incidents'. Consequently, the first Dutch landscapists tended to concentrate on small, intimate scenes or 'close-ups', focusing on a simple motif such as a farm cottage, a frozen river or a row of sandy dunes. In the background they painted low, flat horizons and bleak open skies. To complete this quiet, simple subject-matter, they developed a refined and sophisticated technique, using a subdued palette, with subtle modulations of light and shade.

Ruisdael broke dramatically with the conventions of his predecessors and even his very

The Art Institute of Chicago/Potter Palmer Coll.

A Village in Winter (mid 1660s)

Ruisdael's winter landscape is desolate – a winter to escape from not to enjoy as in the winter skating scenes depicted by other painters. The bleakness of winter is conveyed by the artist's use of monochrome – the only relief from darkness is the dirty white of the snow. The small size and upright format of this picture was characteristic of Ruisdael's winterscapes – a third of them had similar dimensions.

Artothek/Joachim Blauel

Bayerisches Staatsgemäldesammlungen, Munich

early works show little trace of the influence of his uncle, Salomon van Ruysdael. Firstly, Ruisdael painted varied and often novel types of subject-matter. Although like his predecessors, he painted numerous dunescapes, coastal scenes and other 'local' types of landscape, he also painted rolling hills, rocky inclines and foaming waterfalls which bore little relation to what the Dutchman saw around him.

A CREATIVE APPROACH

Secondly, Ruisdael's approach to landscape was freer and more inventive. Although his landscapes were always grounded in observation, Ruisdael rearranged the features of the landscapes he saw into endlessly varied compositions. Most important, Ruisdael deliberately emphasized the picturesque elements in a landscape, and could heighten or dramatize the most ordinary scenes by rich colouring, brilliant lighting effects and strong compositional accents. John Constable, who greatly admired Ruisdael, remarked particularly on this aspect of his work. Describing one of

National Gallery, London

Leipzig, Museum der bildenden Künste

Panoramic View of the Amstel River Looking Towards Amsterdam (late 1670s)

This drawing served as a preliminary study for two paintings. It is an extensive view of Amsterdam seen from the south, probably done from the tower of the Pauwentuin, a popular place on the Amstel river.

Shore at Egmond-aan-Zee

(above) This was painted at the end of Ruisdael's career. The brooding stillness of the seashore scene is broken only by the rolling of the waves. The figures were painted in by Gerard van Battem, who contributed to the mood of the picture by keeping the figures small and muted.

Ruisdael's seascapes, he wrote, 'The subject is the mouth of a Dutch river, without a single feature of grandeur in the scenery; but the stormy sky, the grouping of the vessels and the breaking of the sea, make the picture one of the most impressive ever painted.'

At the beginning of his career, Ruisdael adhered more closely to the traditions of his predecessors. His earliest paintings consist largely of dunescapes, coastal scenes or views of small wooded fields, which focus on a single unremarkable object in the foreground or middle ground. In the *Great Oak* (p.121), for example, the focus of attention is the rugged form of a tree, highlighted by a splash of sunlight.

During the 1650s, Ruisdael began to construct larger, more complex and more spacious views, combining detailed foregrounds with sweeping, distant views, as in the *Hilly Wooded Landscape* (pp.116-17). It was also during this period that he began to paint the exotic, rocky landscapes and waterfalls which became his most popular works, inspired, in part, by his trip to the border regions.

A NEED FOR NEW VISTAS

In itself, Ruisdael's journey to the regions bordering Germany is symptomatic of his approach to landscape. The artists of the previous generation did not feel the need to travel in search of views. They concentrated their attention on the areas around Haarlem and Amsterdam, producing variants on the same motifs. Gradually they evolved different distinct categories of landscape, such as dunescapes, canal scenes or country roads, and concentrated on refining these various genres. Ruisdael, however, felt the need to seek out more complex and challenging views, particularly those which were exotic or picturesque.

Ruisdael's inventiveness is clearly apparent in these scenes, for he continually emphasized the dramatic and atmospheric qualities of the border landscape, playing up the height of the hills and the dimensions of the buildings which took his eye. This is particularly clear in his paintings of the Castle of Bentheim in Westphalia, more than twelve of which survive (p.109). Although the hill on which the castle stands is in fact a low one, Ruisdael painted it as a massive, steep incline, which, together with the rolling skies, gives the castle an almost fairytale appearance. Ruisdael was not primarily concerned with topographical accuracy, but used what he saw as a basis for his own inventions.

The most popular of Ruisdael's works seem to have been his paintings of Scandinavian scenery of which more than 100 survive. Surprising as it may seem, these landscapes were not based on direct observation, for Ruisdael never saw scenery such as this, with its rocky crags, fir trees and cascading waterfalls. Ruisdael's paintings were derived from the works of another Dutch painter, Allart van Everdingen, who had visited Scandinavia and

A Master Draughtsman

Numerous drawings by Ruisdael survive and show him to have been an exceptionally gifted draughtsman. He was particularly skilled at capturing light effects in his drawings, using a mixture of black chalk and wash to create subtle tonal variations. The drawings served a variety of purposes. Many are preparatory studies for paintings, made on the spot and worked up in more detail in the studio, but Ruisdael also made a number of more finished drawings which may have been intended for collectors.

A Windmill and Cottages near a High Footbridge
(above) This drawing of the late 1650s shows an exceptional delicacy of handling. Ruisdael's talent for conveying light effects is particularly noticeable here, especially in his treatment of the river with its glassy surface and shimmering reflections.

Giraudon

Paris, Ecole des Beaux-Arts

The Interior of the Old Church at Amsterdam
(above) This is Ruisdael's only known drawing of an architectural interior and its purpose remains unclear. The Dutch painter Pieter Saenredam specialized in painting church interiors, but they are rare in the works of other artists.

The Shore of the Zuider Zee near Naarden
(right) This drawing cannot be related to any known painting by Ruisdael, although he made several of this area.

Royal Library, Windsor

The Pierpont Morgan Library, New York

Three Half-timbered Houses
(below right) These buildings are typical of those which Ruisdael would have seen during his travels around the West German border region. This drawing was probably made from memory after Ruisdael's return. Buildings of this type feature in many of his works.

Sun-Dappled Trees at the Edge of a Stream (late 1640s)
(right) A distinctive feature of Ruisdael's work is his detailed treatment of trees and foliage. This delicate sketch demonstrates Ruisdael's acute understanding of natural forms.

British Museum

Teylers Museum, Haarlem

COMPARISONS

Landscape Painting

Ruisdael revolutionized the Dutch landscape tradition, substituting grand, dramatic compositions and sweeping chiaroscuro for the small-scale views and subdued tonality of his predecessors. These aspects of Ruisdael's art were highly influential. He was particularly admired by the Romantic landscapists, and his work made a great impact on Constable. Gainsborough shared Ruisdael's taste for picturesque effects, but his landscapes retain a delicacy and restraint which ally him more closely to the work of earlier Dutch landscapists.

National Gallery of Ireland

Thomas Gainsborough (1727-88) **Landscape with Sand Pit** *(above)* *Gainsborough's approach to composition was strongly influenced by the Dutch.*

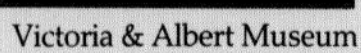

Victoria & Albert Museum

Bridgeman Art Library

John Constable (1776-1837) **Water-Mill at Gillingham** *Constable was a great admirer of Ruisdael. This vigorously painted 'close-up' clearly reflects Ruisdael's influence.*

introduced into Holland the vogue for romantic mountainous landscapes. Everdingen's paintings are often very fine, but Ruisdael went far beyond him in the power and inventiveness of his compositions. Ruisdael's biographer, Arnold Houbraken made particular mention of Ruisdael's waterfalls, noting that 'he could portray water splashing or foaming as it dashed on surrounding rocks so naturally, tenderly and transparently, that it seems to be real water'.

During the 1660s and early 1670s, Ruisdael enlarged his repertoire by painting large, panoramic views such as the *Extensive Landscape* (p.129), and the numerous views of Haarlem and its bleaching fields (p.130). Invariably, Ruisdael enlivened these flat expanses of land by adopting a high view-point, and including strong compositional accents, such as a silhouetted church spire, a sparkling expanse of water, or a brilliantly lit cornfield. He also brought a sense of spaciousness to the view by introducing vast stretches of turbulent sky.

The poetic quality of Ruisdael's landscapes derives primarily from his sensitive use of light

Duke of Buccleuch & Queensberry

Hilly Wooded Landscape with Cattle (early 1650s)
(left and detail above) At this time, Ruisdael became interested in the compositional scheme of hills rising either side of a distant view. Here the geological forms and mass of foliage are emphasized by being close up in the foreground, while the low sky gives the impression of distance. The herdsmen and the cattle are dominated by the landscape. Nonetheless, reflected light illuminates the two figures, drawing attention to them.

and shade. Ruisdael was an acute observer of light and weather conditions, and brought to all his works an unprecedented luminosity. *The Sunlit Grain Field* (p.125), provides a particularly good example of this. Here, Ruisdael has observed with great precision the sweep of a ray of sunlight as it breaks through fast-moving cloud. He also makes a careful distinction between the golden light on the cornfield, and the silvery light which is reflected off the sea.

Ruisdael's use of contrasting light and shade became increasingly dramatic throughout the course of his career, culminating in works such as the magnificent *Coup de Soleil* (p.131). Even in his more subdued winter landscapes (p.128), strong tonal contrasts are used to convey the threatening mood of the snow-laden sky. Constable, the great English landscape painter, wrote: 'Ruisdael . . . delighted in, and has made delightful to our eyes, those solemn days, peculiar to his country and ours, when without storm, large rolling clouds scarcely permit a ray of sunlight to break the shades of the forest. By these effects he enveloped the most ordinary scenes with grandeur.'

TRADEMARKS

Moody Skies

Ruisdael was concerned to create an atmosphere in his landscapes and he did this through his painting of the sky and clouds. He never painted a cloudless sky – and while his range of moods was wide, his particular strong point was the creation of dark, brooding skies, often depicting an impending storm.

THE MAKING OF A MASTERPIECE

The Jewish Cemetery

The Jewish Cemetery is Ruisdael's most poetic and original work. Unusually for Ruisdael, the painting has a clear allegorical significance – the broken tombs, ruined church and blasted tree allude to the notion of *vanitas* – the transience of earthly endeavours. Typically, Ruisdael expresses this idea, not just through symbols, but by creating a distinctive mood – the dark sky, subdued tonality and dense foliage give the painting a solemn, brooding air. At the same time, Ruisdael introduces a note of hope, in the familiar symbol of a rainbow.

Monumental ruins
(left) Ruisdael combines the real and the imaginary in this landscape. The ruins in the background were inspired by the Castle of Egmond.

The graves
The tombs in the painting have all been identified. The central large white tomb is that of Dr Eliahu Montalto, physician to Marie de' Medici. He died in France but was buried at his own request at Ouderkerk.

Staatliche Kunstammlungen, Dresden

Detroit Institute of Arts

'A pure feeling, clear-thinking artist [who] delights, teaches, refreshes and animates . . .'

Goethe

The Jewish Cemetery *(above) In this version there is more light and colour. The rainbow, too, is more visible, emphasizing the renewal of hope. The ruin is based on the Abbey at Egmond.*

Preliminary drawing *This drawing of the Portuguese-Jewish cemetery at Ouderkerk shows an opposite view of the tombs to that in the painting, with St Urban's Church in the distance.*

Teylers Museum, Haarlem

Gallery

Ruisdael usually signed his paintings but he rarely dated them and it is difficult to establish a chronology for his work – the more so because even his earliest pictures are so masterly. He was not only the most powerful of all Dutch landscape painters, but also the most versatile. He could concentrate intensely on a single motif or a

Joachim Blauel/Artothek

Dune Landscape with Plank Fence *c.1650*
17½" × 14½"
Städelsches Kunstinstitut, Frankfurt

There was a particularly strong tradition of dunescape painting in Haarlem, where Ruisdael spent most of his early career, and it is remarkable how so many artists managed to make memorable paintings of such uneventful scenery. Ruisdael's painting is completely unpretentious, but his rich feeling for texture brings it alive.

virtually featureless patch of land, as in The Great Oak and Dune Landscape with Plank Fence, and at the opposite extreme he painted commanding views of almost limitless vistas, as in Extensive Landscape with a Ruined Castle and a Church. And Ruisdael was equally convincing with rustic homeliness (Two Watermills and an Open Sluice) and with visionary grandeur (The Jewish Cemetery). His range in subject matter extended to types of picture that were usually the province of specialists, notably seascapes (Vessels in a Breeze) and winter scenes (Winter Landscape), and in these, too, he showed his unrivalled gifts for depicting the earth and the elements.

Photograph by Courtesy of John Mitchell & Son

The Great Oak *1652*
33½" × 41" On loan to Birmingham City Art Gallery

This painting is signed and dated by Ruisdael, and according to old sources it once also bore the signature (now no longer visible) of Ruisdael's friend Nicolaes Berchem, who painted the figures. This kind of collaboration was common in Dutch painting, particularly with 'staffage' – the term for small figures that are simply animating details.

Deutsche Fotothek, Dresden

The Jewish Cemetery *1650s*
33" × 37½" Gemäldegalerie, Dresden

This is one of two versions of this subject by Ruisdael, and in both pictures he achieved a feeling of tragic intensity very rarely found in landscape painting. The picture is partly based on actual observation of the cemetery at Ouderkerk (some of the tombs can still be recognized today) and partly on invention from the artist's imagination. The work's brooding atmosphere powerfully conveys the notion of the transience of all earthly things.

Photo Christopher Barker

Vessels in a Breeze *late 1650s*
17¾″ × 21½″ National Gallery, London

About 30 seascapes by Ruisdael are known today and it is symptomatic of his preference for showing the dramatic aspects of nature that not one of them features a calm sea. Usually – as here – the paintings are sombre in mood and capture with great conviction the feeling of a chilly and gusty day, with waves roughly breaking on the shore or a breakwater, and the masts of small vessels leaning steeply in the wind.

Two Watermills and an Open Sluice *early 1650s*
34½" × 43¾" National Gallery, London

These watermills were obviously a favourite subject of Ruisdael, for he painted them several times. They belonged to the manor house of Singraven in the province of Overijssel and were also painted by Ruisdael's pupil Hobbema. A feature of Ruisdael's watermill paintings is the mastery with which he portrays the foaming torrents of water, a skill he was to put to more dramatic use when he turned his hand to Scandinavian waterfall scenes.

A Sunlit Grain Field on the Banks of a Coast *early 1660s*
24″ × 28″ Boymans-van Beuningen Museum, Rotterdam

Ruisdael here makes striking use of one of his favourite pictorial devices – showing the sun breaking through heavy clouds to illuminate part of a scene brightly while other parts are in shadow. His mastery of this scheme conveys a vivid sense of the clouds scudding quickly overhead. The site has not been identified with certainty, but it is generally agreed that the sea in the background is the Zuider Zee.

The Windmill at Wijk bij Duurstede *c.1670*
32½″ × 39¾″ Rijksmuseum, Amsterdam

It is perhaps surprising that the windmill, which is the best-known symbol of the Dutch landscape, should appear so infrequently as the major motif in Ruisdael's paintings. However, in this sonorous work, he shows the strength and power of the windmill as it dominates the landscape. It is difficult to ascertain whether this painting has a symbolic meaning, but at the time people were keenly aware of their dependence on the natural forces of wind and water.

A Waterfall *c.1660*
38¾" × 33½" National Gallery, London

The waterfall was a subject that Ruisdael made his own, and he had a particular penchant for Scandinavian torrents, even though he never visited this part of Europe. He began painting these pictures after he moved to Amsterdam in 1656-70. Some of Ruisdael's Scandinavian scenes have a rather bleak, elemental quality, but here there is a fairly calm atmosphere, despite the foaming water.

Winter Landscape *1660s*
16½" × 19¼" Rijksmuseum, Amsterdam

The winter landscape has a long and distinguished history in Netherlandish painting, but in this stark scene Ruisdael broke from the picturesque tradition of showing merry figures tobogganing and skating and painted the true feel of a bleak winter day, with its threatening clouds and forbidding atmosphere. Indeed, several critics have spoken of the 'tragic' nature of the picture, with winter seen as symbolizing sadness and even death.

An Extensive Landscape with a Ruined Castle and a Church
1665-70
43″ × 57½″ National Gallery, London

This is one of Ruisdael's most magnificent extensive views. He painted several pictures showing a similar panorama; they are sometimes called views of Haarlem, but this is incorrect and the scene is presumably largely imaginary. The figures in the left foreground are thought to have been painted by Adriaen van de Velde. There is a smaller version of this picture in the National Gallery, perhaps painted by Ruisdael as a preliminary study.

View of Haarlem with the Bleaching Grounds *1670-5*
21¾" × 24½" Mauritshuis, The Hague

Ruisdael painted this subject several times late in his career, when he was turning more to panoramic views. The bleaching of linen was one of the foundations of Haarlem's prosperity, so the picture can be seen as an expression of Ruisdael's civic pride. He has shown the long strips of cloth lying in the fields to bleach, after being soaked in the spring waters near the dunes. The building in the background is the church of St Bavo, where Ruisdael is buried.

Le Coup de Soleil *1670s*
32½″ × 39″ Louvre, Paris

This imaginary landscape has long been one of Ruisdael's most famous works and the French title (meaning 'the burst of sun') has been current since the early 19th century. It is an extensive view achieving both openness and height. Sunlight bursts through the clouds, accentuating the horizontal river valley and contributing to the sense of drama. The picture was used as a motif on Sèvres porcelain of about 1836.

The Age of Observation

The dawn of the Dutch Republic brought with it a remarkable upsurge of scientific as well as artistic achievement. This was directly related to new needs and new ways of looking at the world.

The importance of astronomy
(below) An astronomer studies a celestial globe on which the constellations are depicted as animals and figures. Astronomy was especially important to 17th-century Dutch seamen, who relied on it for navigational purposes.

For the people of Holland and the other six United Provinces, the Truce of 1609 marked the dawn of a golden age. Released from the yoke of Spanish rule, Dutch merchants had before long made Amsterdam the commercial hub of Europe, and the fortunes of the new republic soared.

The exquisite genre paintings of artists like Vermeer and Ruisdael, and the brilliance of Rembrandt reveal one aspect of the remarkable flowering of Dutch culture in the 17th century. But Dutch achievements in the 100 years after independence extended into many different areas, both intellectual and practical. Dutch scientists were among the most influential of the age and made a number of crucial discoveries. Dutch cartographers set new standards in mapmaking; Dutch engineers were in demand all over Europe for drainage and flood control schemes; Dutch decoration and architecture became the vogue in England; and Dutch sailors were making epic voyages to New Zealand and the far north of Canada. Indeed, there were few corners of the world that did not feel Dutch influence.

What made the United Provinces unique in the 17th century was the way the Dutch people seemed able to apply a practical, down-to-earth approach to everything from painting to growing turnips. To some extent, this practical bent was characteristic of the Protestant revolution that had precipitated the break with Spain. The old Roman Church had laid stress on the mysteriousness of the universe and the assertion that only priests – and ultimately the pope – had access to the truth. It had

Leyden School, National Gallery, London

The centre of anatomy
(right) The Dutch began to study the processes of the human body, and Leyden University became second only to Padua in the study of anatomy. In the anatomy theatre, there were annual public dissections of an executed criminal.

'The Great Boerhaave'
(far right) Professor of Medicine and Chemistry at Leyden University, Hermannus Boerhaave, was also a botanist and mathematician. When lecturing, he stressed the essential simplicity of medicine, and placed it on a sound scientific basis, thereby exploding many alchemical myths.

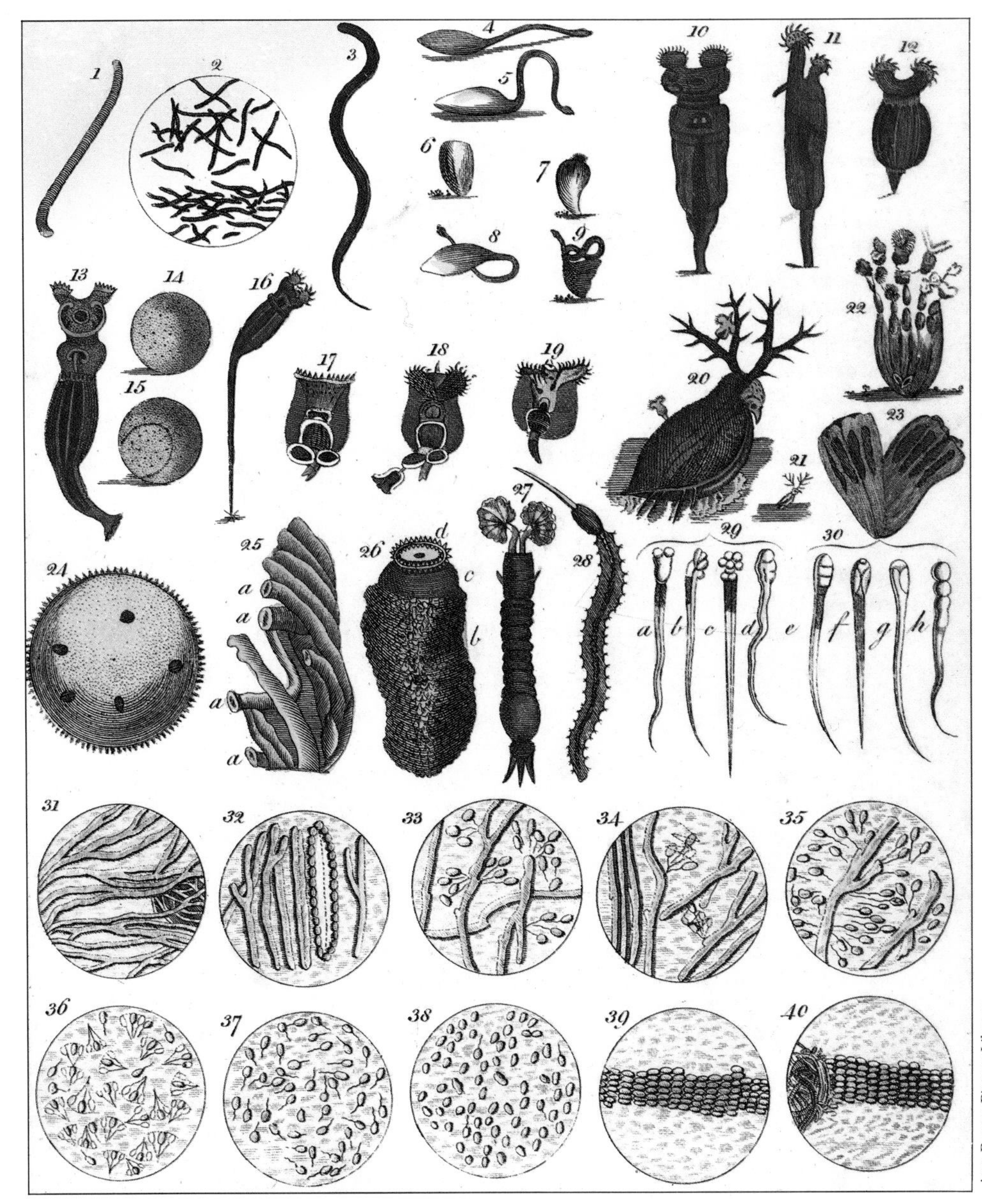

Ann Ronan Picture Library

Mary Evans Picture Library

The pioneer of microscopy
(above and left) Anton van Leeuwenhoek made the first simple microscope by grinding and polishing a lens of sufficiently short focal length to view cells and other minute structures. By this means he was able to give accurate descriptions and make detailed anatomical drawings of blood corpuscles, animal spermatozoa, human muscle, insects and plant organisms (left). In an age when superstition and mumbo jumbo still lingered, Leeuwenhoek's carefully documented experiments and observations were the very essence of scientific research.

Mansell Collection

Detail from 'Boerhave with his Family' by A. de Gelder, Rijksmuseum

also emphasized that it was only the next world that mattered.

The Protestant revolution altered these ideas by stressing that this world is important as a battlefield between good and evil, where every individual's experience counts as much as any church. This appealed very strongly to the Dutch, and they took the new Protestant ideal to heart. It instilled in them a desire to explore everything in the world around them, and gave them confidence in what they saw with their own eyes. Dutch artists and intellectuals began to examine the real world in detail, closely observing even the most mundane phenomena.

While the Dutch genre painters were painting small details of the world around them with superlative skill – interiors, still-lifes and landscapes, rarely thought worthy of the artist's attention before – Dutch scientists began to use lenses to help them see the world better.

The lens was the scientist's most important tool and almost every Dutch scientist could grind and polish his own lenses. Indeed, the great scientist Christiaan Huygens ground lenses professionally. It was the Dutch scientists' ability to exploit lenses,

An eye for detail
(left) Dutch artists as well as scientists shared a fascination for the world around them, and a desire to explore and record it precisely. This showed in the kinds of art they favoured: landscape, genre and still-life. Melchior Hondecoeter was a successful bird painter, and his attention to detail can be seen in this study of bullfinches and butterflies, which even includes a humble toad and snail.

Hondecoeter, National Gallery, London

whether in microscopes or telescopes, that enabled them to make some of the most important discoveries of the century.

At one end of the scale, telescopes of enormous focal length allowed them to see further and further into space. With his own 12 foot focal length telescope, Huygens discovered that the planet Saturn not only had a moon (Titan) but was also encircled by concentric rings. And it was his knowledge of lenses that helped him develop the theory that light travels in waves. At the other end of the scale, Anton van Leeuwenhoek's improved microscope enabled him to confirm, in 1683, Marcello Malphigi's belief that blood from the arteries flowed into tiny capillaries. Later, he discovered tiny corpuscles within the blood, and the existence of micro-organisms (such as bacteria) which he called animalcules.

In keeping with this microscopic examination of the world, 'anatomy' became a vogue word among Dutch intellectuals, and they published books on the *Anatomy of the Universe* and other scientific subjects. The work symbolized the meticulous dissection of a subject which was their aim. Human anatomy became so popular that each year the Guild of Physicians and Surgeons in Leyden would publicly dissect or 'anatomize' the corpse of a recently executed criminal. And the anatomist Hermannus Boerhaave became so famous that he was known simply as 'The Great Boerhaave' and a letter addressed 'Boerhaave, Europe' safely reached him.

The hallmark of Dutch observers of the world, whether artists, astronomers or botanists, was a remarkably methodical approach. They wanted to examine the world in meticulous detail and find out not what purpose, but what process lay behind nature, and mathematics began to assume more and more importance. In keeping with this, the Dutch began to publish instruction books describing the correct method to do anything from painting flowers to grinding lenses.

THE IMPORTANCE OF TRADE

The methodical approach of the Dutch scientists owed a great deal to the Dutch merchant's care in book-keeping and accounting. Life in the United Provinces revolved around trade. Besides focusing attention on the real world, the Protestant revolution had helped to foster the idea that trade and the pursuit of worldly goods were compatible with Christianity – part of the Protestant belief that God rewarded industrious men.

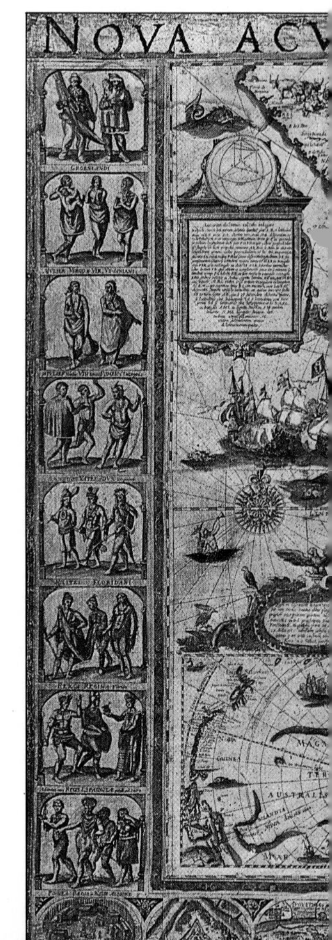

Jan van Goyen, Munich Alte Pinakothek

Joachim Blauel/Artothek

Victoria & Albert Museum

Bridgeman Art Library

Indeed, the Dutch had taken to trade so enthusiastically that the great French philosopher René Descartes, who lived in Amsterdam, grumbled: 'In this great town, . . . apart from myself, there dwells no-one who is not engaged in trade.' And he may not have been exaggerating much, for even scholars and artists often had to trade to support themselves – the painter Jan van Goven, for instance, was a tulip merchant.

Trade not only brought the prosperity that allowed the Dutch to achieve so much, it was the spur to many of these achievements as well. It was trade that impelled many Dutch seamen to undertake voyages into unchartered waters. Heemskerck and Jacob Barentsz were searching for a quicker and cheaper way to the Pacific when they perished in the Arctic sea, while Abel Tasman was looking for a more reliable route to the rich Spanish colonies in South America when he discovered Tasmania (which he called Van Diemen's Land) and New Zealand in the 1640s. And it was to provide sea traders with more reliable information that Dutch mapmakers such as Waghenaer and Willem Jansz Blaeu made their superb charts and inspired an era of superlative mapmaking.

Waghenaer's charts, printed with engraved copper plates, were so successful that for centuries afterwards, British sailors referred to charts as 'waggoners', while the English diarist John Evelyn considered no trip to Amsterdam in the 1640s was complete without a visit to the mapmakers Jodocus Hondius and Blaeu.

The rewards of trade encouraged all kinds of invention and persuaded scientists to look for practical applications for their ideas. It was the need for better navigational equipment to match the expanding sea trade, for instance, that was behind Huygen's invention of the pendulum clock. And the enormous profits that could be made from reclaiming land from the sea spurred on Dutch engineers to develop the skill in drainage that made them so much in demand – not least with the English, soon to be their trading rivals.

A cosmopolitan centre
(above) The flourishing town of Leyden was an important centre of industry and learning. Its famous university attracted students from many countries.

The pendulum clock
(above right) Christiaan Huygens was the first to apply the theory of using a pendulum as part of the timing mechanism of a clock – and so invented the pendulum clock.

Dutch cartography
(below) Discoveries at sea inspired Dutch cartographers to ever higher standards of excellence. Blaeu was one of the most famous, and this map of America was corrected by him.

Tasman's voyages
(right) The navigator, Abel Tasman, discovered Tasmania and New Zealand in the 1640s. His journal includes drawings like this of an encounter with Fijians.

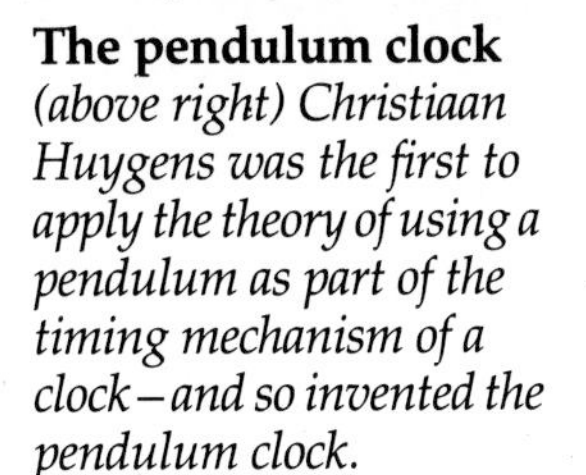

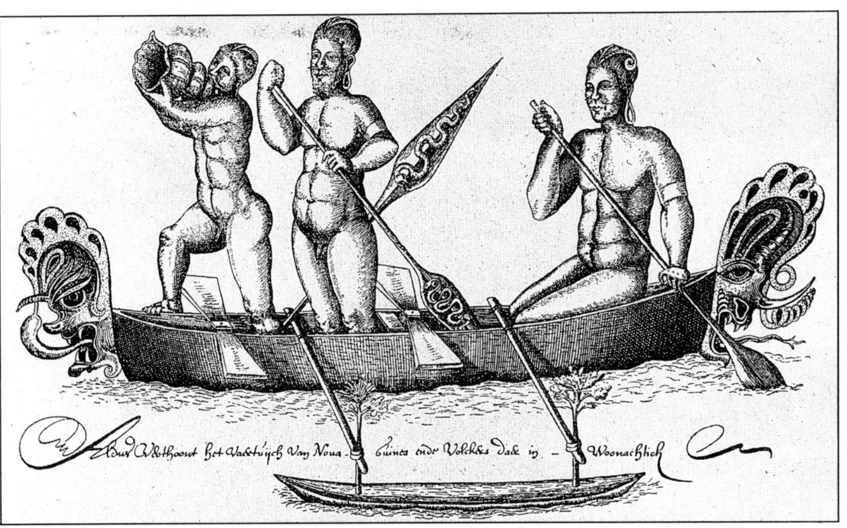

Archiv für Kunst und Geschichte

National Maritime Museum, Greenwich/Michael Holford

A Year in the Life 1648

In 1648, the independence of Ruisdael's native Netherlands was fully recognized and the Thirty Years War finally ended. French ambitions were checked by the outbreak of civil wars known as the Fronde, while in England renewed conflict ensured Cromwell's supremacy and doomed King Charles I.

In January 1648 – two years after Ruisdael was accepted as a member of the Guild of St Luke in Haarlem – Spain and the Dutch Netherlands made peace at Munster, ending eight decades of hostilities. The Spaniards, hard pressed by the revolt of Catalonia and seriously dismayed by French victories in the Netherlands, were ready to buy peace dearly. They not only recognized the independence of their one-time Dutch subjects, but agreed to the closing of the River Scheldt, although this meant the ruin of the remaining Spanish provinces in the Netherlands and the continued commercial supremacy of Dutch Amsterdam.

The Peace of Westphalia in October ended the Thirty Years War, leaving Germany utterly devastated. The Duc d'Enghien (better known by his later title, the Great Condé), had trapped

Dutch independence
(right) The Ratification of the Treaty of Munster, whereby Spain publicly acknowledged Dutch sovereignty in the United Provinces, took place on 15 May 1648 in the Town Hall of the city. In the centre stands Count Peñaranda, the Spanish envoy, who swears his oath while the delegate from the States General of the United Provinces, Barthold van Gent, reads the oath with his right hand raised. On the table lie two caskets containing the Spanish and Dutch copies of the Treaty. The artist, Gerard Terborch, who was an eyewitness to this solemn and historic event, portrayed himself as attentively listening to the proceedings at the far left of the painting.

AISA

G. Westermann/Artothek

Landesgalerie Niedersachs, Hanover

Famous fountain
(left) Built on the site of Domitian's athletic stadium, the Piazza Navona in Rome was elevated to its present Baroque glory by Innocent X. Bernini was pleased to submit a design for the central fountain which had to include an obelisk seen by the Pope on the Appian Way. The Pope was enchanted with the design and work began in 1648 on the Fountain of the Four Rivers, here seen as the centrepiece of an 18th-century water festival.

Scala

and wiped out the Archduke Leopold's Spanish-Imperial army at Lens. At the same time Emperor Ferdinand, having lost Bavaria and on the verge of losing Bohemia, was forced to desert his Spanish relatives and make his peace on terms that ended forever the possibility of making the Holy Roman Empire an effective state. France and Sweden had made important territorial acquisitions inside the Empire, and so gained the right to interfere in its affairs and the independence of the various German states was recognized, along with their right to make treaties with foreign powers without reference to the Emperor.

France on the brink of European primacy was forced to make terms with Spain on the outbreak of the Civil Wars known as the Fronde. A *Fronde* is a sling, and the first *Frondeurs* were, among other things, stone throwers, protesting against higher taxes. The grievances of the Paris mob were exploited by opponents of the government, notably the nobles and *Parlements* (courts of appeal, which resented the centralizing policy of the monarchy). At this point the crown was relatively weak, since Louis XIV was still a minor and France was ruled by the Italian-born Cardinal Mazarin in the name of the regent, who was Louis' mother, Anne of Austria.

CIVIL WARS

The first act of the Fronde occurred while Paris was still celebrating the victory of Lens. The government tried to arrest leading trouble-makers in the Paris *Parlement*, only to find itself

Bildarchiv Preussischer Kulturbesitz

Invasion of Bohemia
(left) A Swedish army under Königsmarck invaded Bohemia in July 1648 and succeeded in capturing the suburb of Prague where the treasures of the Holy Roman Emperor Rudolph II (1552-1612) had been housed. Books, paintings and works of art were seized and sent back to Stockholm to join similar booty looted during Sweden's involvement in the war. The current Emperor, Ferdinand III, faced with the imminent prospect of losing all Bohemia, was thus finally forced to put his name as a signatory to the Peace of Westphalia and end the Thirty Years War.

Victory at Lens
(right) France had been at war with Spain since 1635 and despite the European peace of 1648, the struggle would continue another 11 years. France was fortunate to have as general the Prince de Condé who had already won brilliant victories against seeming impossible odds. On 10 August, he led his army against the Archduke Leopold who was beseiging Lens in Artois. Although outnumbered, the Prince scattered the Spanish and Imperial troops, killing 3000 and taking 5000 prisoner.

Bulloz

Versailles

Louvre, Paris

Elegant city hall
(left) Work began on the new Stadhuis *or city hall of Amsterdam on 20 January 1648. Designed by Jacob van Campen (1595-1657), whose work was much influenced by Italian classicism, the building was not completed until 1705. Built to house the bureaucratic machinery of a bourgeois city state, it is ironic that a century and a half later the* Stadhuis *was turned into a royal palace under Louis Bonaparte, and then the Orange dynasty.*

faced by a general uprising. Mazarin hastily backed down and made wide-ranging concessions to avoid weakening France's international position until peace was concluded at Westphalia. Then, in January 1649, the entire Court slipped out of Paris and, joined by the Great Condé, laid siege to the rebel city. The ensuing civil wars were to last more than four years.

In England, the Civil War between Charles I and Parliament, which had been lost by the King, had been a relatively gentlemanly affair, but the second Civil War of 1648 was a harsher business. Charles, though a prisoner, had remained free to negotiate a settlement with Parliament and the Army but by this time his evasions and deceptions (he was playing for time) were wearing out their patience. As he had hoped , the uncertainties of the situation had caused a reaction in his favour in several parts of England. He had also made a secret alliance with the Scots, who prepared to invade as the first royalist risings took place in April and May.

Though stretched to the utmost, the army crushed or contained the royalists in Wales, Kent, Essex and the north. The Scots arrived too late and, badly led by the Duke of Hamilton, were destroyed by numerically inferior forces led by Cromwell in a series of actions between Preston and Wigan.

With the royalist collapse complete, the Army took control of the King and Parliament was subjected to 'Pride's Purge', whereby undesirable members were ejected under the supervision of Colonel Pride. The remaining, politically reliable 'Rump' ordered the trial of the King. On 30 January 1649, Charles I ended his life on the scaffold.

The regency
(right) On Louis XIII's death in 1643, his wife Anne of Austria became absolute regent with the increasingly unpopular Cardinal Mazarin as her chief minister. Her two sons, Louis XIV and Philippe, Duc d'Anjou, who are seen here kneeling to the left of the Queen, were ten and eight-years-old respectively in 1648. It was a year which saw the beginning of a series of civil wars. The Paris Parlement, *encouraged by revolts in England, Naples and Catalonia, declared against high taxation and the centralizing policies of Mazarin. In October the Crown was forced to accede to the Declaration of St Germain, making the monarchy constitutional, but it never came into force. These were dark days for the young Louis, whose fanatical absolutism as* Le Roi Soleil *was probably due to fears of another series of civil wars or Frondes.*

Lauros-Giraudon

Versailles

Popular uprising
(left) The French Queen arrested four of the leading dissenters in Parlement *and the people of Paris rioted. For two days the capital city was in uproar and the barricades were out for the second, but by no means the last, time in French history. The fighting stopped when the members were freed, but the Court left the city in January 1649. Soon afterwards Paris was beseiged by the Prince de Condé in support of the Queen.*

Jean-Loup Charmet

Bibliotheque Nationale

GALLERY GUIDE

Caravaggio

The best selection of Caravaggio's work is to be found in Rome, both in public galleries and in local churches. Of the former, the best endowed is the Borghese Gallery, with its remarkable depictions of David (p.35) and St. Jerome, while further examples can be found in the Vatican (p.32) and the Galleria Doria-Pamphili (p.25). Prominent among the churches are S. Luigi dei Francesi, with its three dramatic scenes from the Life of St Matthew (pp.14 and 20-21) and the Cerasi Chapel in Santa Maria del Popolo (pp.30-31). Elsewhere, there are major works in London (pp.28-9), in Paris (pp.24 and 34) and in Florence (pp.18 and 26). Caravaggio is also well-represented in American collections, most notably at the Wadsworth Athenaeum, Hartford, Connecticut *(The Ecstasy of St Francis)*, the Cleveland Museum of Art, Cleveland, Ohio *(The Crucifixion of St Andrew)* and the Metropolitan Museum of Art, New York *(The Musicians)*.

Velázquez

As a result of Philip IV's lifelong patronage, the greatest collections of Velázquez's paintings are to be found at the Prado, Madrid, and at the Escorial. He is well-represented in London, too, both at the National Gallery, which contains his celebrated nude, *The Rokeby Venus* (pp.62-3), and at the Wellington Museum, where striking examples of his early, naturalistic style are on display (p.57). There are excellent portraits in Boston *(Luis de Gongora* – the Museum of Fine Arts) and New York (p.64). The latter also houses one of Velázquez's finest religious paintings, *Christ at Emmaus* (Metropolitan Museum of Art).

Van Dyck

Van Dyck's fame rests principally on the superb series of portraits that he produced under the patronage of Charles I and, not surprisingly, the richest selection of these is to be found in the Royal Collection in London (pp.92, 94-5, 96-7). However, he did not work exclusively for the King and many country houses still possess their family portraits. Outside England, Van Dyck's portrait style is best represented at the Louvre, the National Gallery of Art, Washington (p.93) and at the Frick Collection in New York. His religious and mythological scenes are more widely dispersed. The strongest collection of the former is at the Prado, Madrid (p.88) and there are further interesting examples in Vienna (Kunsthistorisches Museum) and in Indianapolis (John Herron Art Museum).

Ruisdael

The widespread popularity of Ruisdael, combined with his large output, have ensured that most major collections have an example of his work. Most famous are the solemn, brooding landscapes that prefigure the Romantic movement and the definitive examples of these are the two versions of *The Jewish Cemetery* (pp.118-19, Dresden and Detroit) and the *Ruins of the Castle of Egmond* (pp.112-13, Chicago, Art Institute). Ruisdael was also particularly adept at depicting the turbulent flow of water, and stormy seascapes and waterfalls were both favourite subjects. The latter are most extensively represented in the National Gallery in London (pp.124 and 127), while American collections are rich in the former (the best examples being at the Boston Museum of Fine Arts and the Worcester Art Museum).

BIBLIOGRAPHY

G. Bazin, *Baroque and Rococo*, Thames & Hudson, New York, 1985

W. Friedlaender, *Caravaggio Studies*, Princeton University Press, Princeton, 1974

J. Gash, *Caravaggio*, Hippocrene Books, New York, 1981

E. Harris, *Velázquez*, Cornell University Press, Ithaca, 1982

H. Hibbard, *Caravaggio*, Harper & Row, New York, 1983

M. Levey, *Ruisdael*, National Gallery Publications, London, 1977

J. Lopez-Rey, *Velázquez's Work and World*, Faber & Faber, London, 1968

O. Millar, *Van Dyck in England*, National Portrait Gallery, London, 1982

J. Muller, *Velázquez*, Thames & Hudson, New York, 1976

S. Slive and H. Hoetink, *Jacob van Ruisdael*, Abbeville Press, New York, 1981

P. Troutman, *Velázquez*, Spring Books, Hamlyn, London, 1965

E. Waterhouse, *Italian Baroque Painting*, Phaidon, London, 1962

R. Wittkower, *Art and Architecture in Italy: 1600-1750*, Viking Press, New York, 1959

OTHER BAROQUE ARTISTS

Gianlorenzo Bernini (1598-1680)
Italian sculptor, painter and architect; the presiding genius of the Baroque. Born in Naples, the son of a Tuscan sculptor who moved to Rome in c.1605, Bernini was precociously talented and soon outgrew the Mannerist limitations of his father's art. His statues for Cardinal Borghese (1618-25) already displayed a restless energy and realism, and reflected his admiration for the paintings of Annibale Carracci and Caravaggio. Under the papacy of Urban VIII (1623-44), Bernini won a series of prestigious commissions, including the design of the Baldacchino for St Peter's (1624-33) and the restoration of Santa Bibbiana. However, his greatest gift was for sculpture and in The Ecstasy of St Theresa *(1645-52, Cornaro Chapel, Sta Maria della Vittoria) he produced his masterpiece, a vision of helpless rapture that has become one of the central images of the Baroque movement. He excelled as a portrait sculptor and his few paintings – executed, it appears, solely for his own amusement – are also of a very high quality.*

Pietro da Cortona (1596-1669)
The major decorative painter of the High Baroque. Born Pietro Berrettini, the son of a stone-mason, he moved from Cortona to Rome in c.1612 and began working in a loosely classical style. His first important commission was for the frescoes at Santa Bibbiana – Bernini's first architectural project. Contact with the latter seems to have encouraged Pietro to instil a greater sense of movement and dynamism into his work, and this bore fruit in his illusionistic masterpiece, the ceiling decorations at the Palazzo Barberini (1633-9). In 1637, he visited Venice, where the example of Veronese and others contributed to a general lightening of his palette and resulted in the richly decorative designs of his ceiling in the Palazzo Pamphili (1651-4), with its prefiguration of the Rococo style. Pietro's easel paintings were unremarkable, but he enjoyed a successful career as an architect.

William Dobson (1610-46)
The greatest English-born painter of the 17th century. Dobson was the son of a minor government official and the rudimentary information known about his early years suggests that his training was conducted by William Peake and Francis Cleyn. However, the greatest influence on his style was the superb royal art collection – dominated by the Venetians and Van Dyck – which Charles I had assembled at the Palace of Whitehall. Dobson followed the king to his Civil War capital at Oxford and became Court Painter upon the death of Van Dyck. Almost all his surviving works date from this Civil War period (1642-6).

Orazio Gentileschi (1563-1639)
Italian painter, one of the principal followers of Caravaggio. Gentileschi was born in Pisa but soon moved to Rome, where he worked initially in a Mannerist style. He came under the influence of Caravaggio after 1600, but adapted his methods into a gentler, more lyrical vision. Through his travels –

The Birth of the Virgin
(below) This painting, begun in 1655, is an early example of Bartolomé Esteban Murillo's break with the naturalistic tradition of Spanish religious work.

he visited Genoa, France and England – Gentileschi disseminated the lessons of Caravaggism, although these became increasingly diluted at the end of his career. He eventually settled in London, where his most important commission was for the Queen's House at Greenwich.

Luca Giordano (1634-1705)

The major Neapolitan painter of the late 17th century, who earned a reputation for speed and versatility. His early work drew heavily on the realism of Caravaggio and Ribera, but this was superseded by an admiration for the colouristic brilliance of the Venetians. He succeeded Pietro da Cortona as the most respected of the Baroque decorators and his greatest achievements in this field were the ceiling frescoes at the Escorial.

Il Guercino (1591-1666)

Remarkable Italian artist from Cento, near Bologna. Born Giovanni Barbieri (Guercino means 'squint-eyed'), he was initially influenced by the painterly classicism of Ludovico Carracci but soon modified this, introducing bold tonal contrasts and a freedom of handling that clearly derived from Caravaggio. These spirited qualities were evident in his most celebrated work, the Aurora, *in the Casino Ludovisi (1621-3).*

Meindert Hobbema (1638-1709)

Dutch landscape painter, based in Amsterdam. Hobbema was a close friend and pupil of Jacob van Ruisdael and many of their works from the late 1650s are almost indistinguishable. Increasingly, though, he abandoned his mentor's dramtic themes to concentrate on peaceful, sunlit scenes, typified by his celebrated Avenue at Middelharnis *(p.111, National Gallery, London). In 1668, he became a Customs official and thereafter neglected his painting. Hobbema's reputation was limited during his lifetime but grew enormously in the 19th century, when his informal compositions exerted a profound influence on the English and French landscape painters.*

Georges de La Tour (1593-1652)

The most gifted and individual of Caravaggio's followers. La Tour was born and worked in the French province of Lorraine. His early naturalistic style was marked by strong chiaroscuro effects that were probably learned from members of the Utrecht School, such as Terbrugghen and Honthorst. La Tour soon abjured the dynamic qualities of his sources, however, to evolve a more passive and simplified style. The resulting religious images were both intensely moving and exuded a serene grandeur. Nonetheless, his artistic isolation led to his work being neglected for centuries after his death.

Bartolomé Esteban Murillo (1618-82)

Popular Spanish painter whose art represents the last flowering of the Baroque. Murillo was born in Seville, where he achieved early renown with his paintings for the cloisters of the San Francisco monastery, and rapidly superseded Zurburan as the city's leading artist. To modern eyes, Murillo's most interesting works date from this youthful period, when he was clearly affected by the astringent naturalism of Ribera and Velázquez. Increasingly, however, he developed his estilo vaporoso, *in which his preferred subjects – Madonnas and beggar-boys – were sweetened and sentimentalized through the use of a lyrical palette and feathery draughtsmanship. This earned him immense popularity in the 18th century, particularly with Rococo artists like Boucher, and encouraged workshops to continue producing pastiches of Murillo until the 19th century. His reputation has declined in modern times.*

Jusepe de Ribera (1591-1652)

Important figure linking the Italian and Spanish Baroque traditions. Ribera was born in Jativa, near Valencia, where he may have trained under Ribalta before leaving for Italy. There, he enjoyed a bohemian existence before settling in Naples in 1616. The city was then under the rule of Spanish Viceroys and they became Ribera's most important patrons, bringing him fame both at home and abroad. Ribera's harsh early style owed much to Caravaggio, but this mellowed after 1630, perhaps reflecting the influence of Velázquez.

Hendrick Terbrugghen (1588-1629)

Dutch painter; a leading member of the Utrecht School, which transmitted Caravaggio's influence into Holland. Terbrugghen was born in Deventer and trained under Bloemaert, but the crucial influence on his style came from his stay in Rome (1604-14), at a time when Caravaggio's reputation was at its peak. In particular, he borrowed from the master's treatment of light and his unusual choice of subject-matter.

Sir James Thornhill (1675/6-1734)

The only major British-born exponent of the grand Baroque tradition. Thornhill learnt his trade from the example of Verrio and Laguerre, and his career coincided with the brief vogue in England of large-scale decorative painting. His greatest achievement in this vein was the enormous Painted Hall at Greenwich Hospital, (now the Royal Naval College), London, with its ambitious symbolic programme.

Juan de Valdés Leal (1622-90)

Important Spanish painter whose work best represents the pessimistic side of the Baroque movement. Valdés Leal was active mainly in his native Seville, where he produced the stunning series on Death and Judgment *for the Hospital of Charity. These renowned pictures form a striking contrast to the refined style of his contemporary, Murillo, illustrating the artist's preference for macabre subjects, characterized by dramatic lighting and almost 'expressionist' brushwork.*

Francisco Zurburan (1598-1664)

One of the leading Spanish Tenebrist painters. Zurburan was born near Badajoz but worked mainly in Seville, where he became a friend of Velázquez. The austere realism of his paintings of saints accorded well with the monastic ideals which the Counter-Reformation sought to promote and he made a career of exporting these devotional works to religious houses in the Spanish colonies of South America. Zurburan's stark lighting effects were patently derived from Caravaggio although, unlike the latter, his figures seemed drained of emotion.

INDEX

Note Page numbers in italic type refer to illustrations.

A

Adoration of the Magi, The (Velázquez) 45
Adoration of the Shepherds (La Tour) *38-9*
'anatomy', 17th-century study of *132-3,* 134
Anguissola Sofonista *80*
Anne of Austria 137, 138
apprenticeships: Caravaggio's 12
Van Dyck's 76
Velázquez's 44-5
Aratori, Lucia 12
Archangel Michael, The (Reni) *105*
Arpino, Cavaliere d' *12,* 13
Artist's Family, The (Velázquez) *48*
astronomy, in the 17th century *132-3,* 134
Avenue at Middleharnis, The (Hobbema) *111*

B

Baburen, Dirck van 39
Bacchus (Caravaggio) *18*
backgrounds: Caravaggio's use of 20
Van Dyck's use of 82, 83
Bacon, Francis: *Pope I 52*
Baglione, Giuseppe 14-15, 17, 39
Life of Caravaggio 14
Balen, Hendrick van 76
Beheading of St John the Baptist (Caravaggio) 16, *16, 18-19*
Bellori: on Caravaggio 16
on Van Dyck 78, 79, 80-81
Bernini, Gianlorenzo 140
Bust of Charles I (copy) *87*
Fountain of the Four Rivers 136
St Peter's Square *72*
Blasted Elm with View of Edmond aan Zee (Ruisdael) *9*
Boar Hunt (Velázquez) *68-9*
bodegones 50-51
Boschini, Marco, on Velázquez 47
Brueghel, Jan: *Isobel of Bourbon* (collab, with Velázquez) *69*
Bruno, Giordano 40, *40*
Buen Retiro, Madrid 68-9, 70, *70-71*
Buffoon Juan de Calabazas, The (Velázquez) *52, 53*
Bullfinches and Butterflies (Hondecoeter) *134*
Bust of Charles I (copy, Bernini) *87*

C

Calling of St Matthew, The (Caravaggio) *20-21*
Calling of St Matthew (Pareja) *49*
Campen, Jacob van: *Stadhuis, Amsterdam 137*
Caracciolo, Giovanni Battista 37
The Liberation of St Peter 37
Caravaggio (Michelangelo Merisi) *9, 11*
apprenticeship 12
and d'Arpino *12,* 13
arrests 15
and backgrounds 20
beginning of success 14
behaviour 14
bias against 39
birthplace 12-13
and Cesari 13
and chiaroscuro 20, *20*
commissions: for Chiesa del Monte della Misericordia 37
for Chiesa Nuova 19-20
for Contarelli Chapel 14, *14,* 19
for Del Monte *14*
papal 12
rejection of religious 21
in court 14-15, *15*
criticism of 21
death of 17
and Del Monte 13
disregard for convention 18-21
drawings 21
early training *18*
family 12
and fresco-painting 21
fight at the Campo Marco 16
finances, in Rome 13
followers *see* Caravaggisti, The
friends and companions 15
and Gentileschi 36
in hospital 13
influence on 17th-century art 36, 39
inheritance 12
key dates 13
and the Knights of Malta 16-17, *16-17*
last days 17
by Leoni *36*
life-style 14, 44
in Malta *16,* 16-17
and Marino 15
mistress 13, 15
models 13, *15,* 21
in Naples 16, *16-17,* 17
influence of style in 37-9
and the Old Masters 16
papal pardon for 16, 17
patrons 13, 15
and perspective 20
and Peterzano 12
in prison 17
in Rome *12,* 12-13, 16-17
sexuality 13
in Sicily 17, *37*
style: and Counter-Reformation's traditions 18-19
criticisms of 21
followers and 36-9
most striking feature 20-21, 36
naturalism of 18-21
use of light 20-21, 36
subjects of early paintings 13
technique 21
trademarks 20
works: comparisons with 'high art' 21
effect of modern illumination on 20
sense of violence in 18
works by:
Bacchus 18
Beheading of St John the Baptist 16, *16, 18-19*
Calling of St Matthew, The 20-21
Conversion of St Paul, The 21, *30*
Crucifixion of St Peter, The 31
David with the Head of Goliath 35
Death of the Virgin, The 17, 21, *24, 36-7*
Entombment of Christ, The 19-20, *32*
Gipsy Fortune Teller, The 24
Grandmaster Alof de Wignacourt 16, *17*
Judith Beheading Holofernes 18, *27*
Madonna di Loreto, The 33
Madonna dei Palafrenieri (detail) *15*
Martyrdom of St Matthew 14
Medusa 19
Musicians, The 14
Raising of Lazarus, models for 21
Rest on the Flight into Egypt, The 25
Sacrifice of Abraham, The 18, *26*
self-portrait *11*
as Bacchus *13*
Seven Works of Mercy 37
Still-Life 18, 21
Supper at Emmaus 19, 22, *22-3, 28-9*
Victorious Cupid 13, *19*
Caravaggisti, The 36-9
Carducho, Vincenzo 39
Castle at Bentheim, The (Ruisdael) *109*
Castle of Egmond, Ruisdael and *108-109, 112-13*
Cesari, Giuseppe 13
Charles I, King of England *69, 100,* 100-103, 104-105, 138
Eikon Basilike, The 103
as patron of the arts 102
and Van Dyck 79
Charles I on Horseback with Seigneur de St Antoine (Van Dyck) *92*
Charles I in Three Positions (Van Dyck) *86, 87, 94-5*
Chastisement of Cupid, The (Manfredi) *37*
chiaroscuro, Caravaggio and 20, *20*
Christ before the High Priest (Honthorst) *39*
Christ Crowned with Thorns (Van Dyck) *88*
Constable, John: on Ruisdael's landscape 113-14, 117
Water-mill at Gillingham 116
Contarelli Chapel *14,* 19
Conversation Piece (Ruisdael, with Keyser) *109*
Conversion of St Paul, The (Caravaggio) 21, *30*
Cortona, Pietro da 140
Counter-Reformation 13-14, 18-19
Coup de Soleil, Le (Ruisdael) 112, 117, *131*
Court Fool 'El Primo', The (Velázquez) *60*
Court Fool Sebastián de Morra, The (Velázquez) *61*
Crucifix (sculpture, Montañés) *46*
Crucifixion of St Peter, The (Caravaggio) *31*
Cupid and Psyche (Van Dyck) *98*

D

David with the Head of Goliath (Caravaggio) *35*
Death of the Virgin (Caravaggio) 17, 21 *34, 36-7*
Dobson, William 140
Dune Landscape with Plank Fence (Ruisdael) *120*
Dyck, Anthony van *see* Van Dyck, Anthony

E

Elizabeth I, Queen of England *40,* 41
Emperor Theodosius Refused Entry into Milan Cathedral, The (Rubens) *78*
Emperor Theodosius Refused Entry into Milan Cathedral, The (Van Dyck) *79*
England 72-3, 100, 103
Civil War in *102-103,* 138
portraiture in 17th-century 83-4
tastes of collectors in 17th-century 79
Entombment of Christ, The (Caravaggio) 19-20, *32*
Esclavo, El *see* Pareja, Juan de
etching, Ruisdael and 111
Everdingen, Allart van *110*
Ruisdael and 114
Expulsion of the Moriscos, The (Velázquez) 46
Extensive Landscape with a Ruined Castle and a Church, An (Ruisdael) 112, 116, *129*

F

Five Children of Charles I (Van Dyck) *83, 96-7*
Forge of Vulcan, The (Velázquez) 48
Fountain of the Four Rivers (sculpture, Bernini) *136*
France: the regency in 137-8, *138*
17th-century territorial gains 137
war with Spain 71, 72-3
François Langlois (Van Dyck) *82-3*
fresco-painting, Caravaggio and 21

G

Gainsborough, Thomas: influence of Van Dyck 82
Landscape with Sand Pit 116
Gaspar de Guzman, Count of Olivares (Velázquez) *68*
Gentileschi, Artemisia 37-8
Judith and Holofernes 38
self-portrait *38*
Gentileschi, Orazio 36, 140-41
The Rest on the Flight into Egypt 36-7

'Gerard of the Night Scenes' *see* Honthorst, Gerrit van
Giordano, Luca 141
Giorgione, technique 21
Gipsy Fortune Teller, The (Caravaggio) *24*
Giustiniani, Marchese 15
Góngora, Luis de (Velázquez) *45*, 46
Gonzaga, Cardinal Ferdinando, and Caravaggio 17
Goyen, Jan van 108, 112
Graeff, Cornelis de 111
Grandmaster Alof de Wignacourt (Caravaggio) 16, *17*
Great Oak, The (Ruisdael) 114, *121*
Grimaldi, Marchesa Elena *82*
Guercino, Il 141
Guild of St Luke, Antwerp, Van Dyck and 76, 77
Guild of St Luke, Haarlem 108
Ruisdael and 109, 136
Guzman, Don Gaspar de (Olivares) 69, 70-71
and Velázquez 46, *68*

H

Henrietta Maria (Van Dyck) *87*, *101*
Henrietta Maria, Queen of England 85, 102
Herrera the Elder, Francesco de 44
'high art', comparison of Caravaggio's works with 21
Hilly Landscape with Cattle (Ruisdael) 114, *116-17*
Hobbema, Meindart 141
The Avenue at Middleharnis 111
Holland/United Provinces 132-135
Hollar, Wenceslaus: on Van Dyck's mistress 81
Lucas and Cornelis de Wael (after Van Dyck) *79*
homosexuality, Caravaggio and 13
Hondecoeter, Melchior: *Bullfinches and Butterflies 134*
Honthorst, Gerrit van 39
Christ before the High Priest 39
Houbraken, Arnold 109, 116
Huygens, Christiaan *73*, 133, 134, *135*

I

Immaculate Conception, The (Velázquez) 45, 51, *56*
Infanta Margarita, The (Velázquez) *54*
Infanta Margarita in Blue, The (Velázquez) *67*
Innocent X (Velázquez) 53, *65*
Innocent X, Pope, and Velázquez *48*
instruction books, 17th-century 134
Interior of the Old Church at Amsterdam, The (drawing, Ruisdael) *114*
Isabel of Bourbon (Velázquez/ Jan Brueghel) *69*

J

Jewish Cemetery, The (Ruisdael) 112 *118-19*, *122*
Jordaens, Jacob, commissions from Charles I 81
Joseph's Coat (Velázquez) 48
Juan de Pareja (Velázquez) *64*
Judith Beheading Holofernes (Caravaggio) 18, *27*
Judith and Holofernes (A. Gentileschi) *38*

K

Keyser, Thomas de 111
Conversation Piece (with Ruisdael) *109*
Knight of the Golden Fleece (Rubens) *85*
Knights of Malta, and Caravaggio 16, *16-17*

L

Lady Elizabeth Thimbleby and Dorothy, Viscountess Andover (Van Dyck) *99*
landscape/landscapists:
comparisons of 116, *116*
Dutch 108, 112, 114
van Goyen and 112
Isaack van Ruisdael and 108
Ruisdael and 112-14, 116-17
Ruysdael and 108
Van Dyck and *79*, 82
van de Velde and 112
Landscape with a River by a Wood (Vroom) *108-109*
Landscape with the Ruins of the Castle of Egmond (Ruisdael) *112-13*
Landscape with Sand Pit (Gainsborough) *116*
Landscape with Waterfall by a Cottage (J. S. Ruisdael) *110*
Landseer, Sir Edwin: *Queen Victoria at Osborne 85*
La Tour, Georges de 39, 141
Adoration of the Shepherds 38-9
Le Valentin: *Soldiers Playing Dice 36-7*
Leeuwenhoek, Anton van *133*, 134
Lemon, Margaret 81
by Van Dyck *78*
Leonardo da Vinci 16
Leoni, Ottavio: drawing of Caravaggio *36*
Liberation of St Peter, The (Caracciolo) *37*
light/shade: Caravaggio's use of 20-21, 36
Ruisdael's use of 116-17
Van Dyck's use of 84-5
Lomellini Family,The (Van Dyck) *82*, 83
Lord John and Lord Bernard Stuart (Van Dyck) *84*
Lotto, Lorenzo: *Triple Portrait of a Jeweller 87*
Louis XIV, King of France 49, 137, *138*
Louis and Rupert of the Rhine (Van Dyck) *102-103*
Lucas and Cornelis de Wael (Hollar, after Van Dyck) *79*

M

Madonna di Loreto, The (Caravaggio) *33*
Madonna dei Palafrenieri (detail, Caravaggio) *15*
maestro pintor de ymagineria, Velázquez as 45
Mander, Karel van 14, 19
Manfredi, Bartolommeo 37
Chastisement of Cupid, The 37
Marchesa Elena Grimaldi (Van Dyck) *82*
Margaret Lemon (Van Dyck) *78*
Marie de Raet (Van Dyck) *91*
Marino, Giovanni Battista 15
Martyrdom of St Matthew (Caravaggio) 14
Mary Ruthven (Van Dyck) *81*
Medusa (Caravaggio) *19*
Meninas, Las (Velázquez) 49, 53, *54* *54*, *55*, *66*
Merisi, Fermo di Bernardino 12
Merisi, Michelangelo *see* Caravaggio
Michelangelo, Caravaggio and 16
microscopes/microscopy, 17th-century 133, 134
Mocenigo, Giovanni 40
Montañés, Juan Martinez: *Crucifix 46*
Murillo, Bartolomé Esteban *71*, 141
Mus, Decius, commission for Rubens 77
Musicians, The (Caravaggio) *14*
Mytens, Daniel 83-4

N

Nicholas Lanier (Van Dyck) *80*
nudes, Veláquez's only 48, *62-3*

O

Old Woman Frying Eggs (Velázquez) *50*
Olivares, Count of *see* Guzman, Don Gaspar de
Ospidale della Consolazione 13

P

Pacheco, Francisco 44-5, 46, 47, 50
Art of Painting, The 50
St John on Patmos (after Velázquez) *44*
Pacheco, Juana, and Velázquez 45
Palomino, Antonio 44, 47, 48, 49, 50-51
Panoramic View of the Amstel River Looking Towards Amsterdam (Ruisdael) *112-13*
Pareja, Juan de 48, 53, *64*
Baptism of Christ, The 48
Calling of St Matthew, The 49
self-portrait *49*
Pembroke Family, The (Van Dyck) 84
perspective, Caravaggio and 20
Peterzano, Simone 12
Philip IV (Velázquez) *51*, *68*
Philip IV, King of Spain 68-71
and Velázquez 46
Philippe le Roy, Seigneur de Ravels (Van Dyck) *90*
Pool Surrounded by Trees, A (Ruisdael) *112*
Pope I (Bacon) *52*
Pope Innocent X (Velázquez) *65*
Pope Paul III (Titian) *52*
Portrait of Elena Grimaldi (Van Dyck) 78, *78*
Prince Baltasar Carlos (Velázquez) *70*
Prince Philip Prosper (Velázquez) *53*
Prince William of Orange and Princess Mary Stuart (Van Dyck) *83*
'props', Van Dyck's use of 84

Q

Queen Henrietta Maria with her Dwarf Sir Jeffrey Hudson (Van Dyck) *93*
Queen Victoria at Osborne (Landseer) *85*

R

Raising of Lazarus (Caravaggio) 21
Raphael, Caravaggio and 16
Ratification of the Treaty of Munster (Terborch) *136*
Reni, Guido 37
Archangel Michael, The 105
Rest on the Flight into Egypt (Caravaggio) *25*
Rest on the Flight into Egypt, The (Gentileschi) *36-7*
Rest on the Flight into Egypt, The (Van Dyck) *89*
Reynolds, Joshua 82
Ribera, Jusepe de 38, 47-8, 141
Rinaldo and Armida (Van Dyck) 79, *81*
River Landscape (S. van Ruysdael) *110*
Rokeby Venus, The (Velázquez) 50, *62-3*
Rome 12, 13-14
Rubens, Sir Peter Paul *46*, 47, 77, 80, 85
Emperor Theodosius Refused Entry into Milan Cathedral, The 78
Knight of the Golden Fleece, The 85
self-portrait *47*
Stage of Welcome 106
Ruisdael, Isaack van 108
Ruisdael, Jacob van *9*, *107*
in Amsterdam *110*, 11
artistic background 108
baptism of 111
and Castle of Bentheim *108-109*, *112-13*, 114
collaboration with Keyser 111
death of 111
as doctor of medicine 109-110, *110-11*
draughtsmanship 114-15, *114-15*
early influences on 108
early training 108, 109
family 108, 110, *110*
finances, for his father 111
and Guild of St Luke, Haarlem 136
influence of Everdingen 114
influence of Vroom *108-109*
key dates 108
and landscape 112-14, 116-17
and light/shade 116-17
and the open market 111
patrons 111
publishes etching 111
pupil 111
and S. van Ruysdael 108
search for inspiration *108-109*
style, treatment of water 116
subjects 113, 114, 116
and Sweerts 111
trademarks 117
travels 110, 114
use of high view-point 116
wills 111
works 109, 114
works by:
Blasted Elm with a View of Edmond aan Zee 9
Castle at Bentheim, The 109
Conversation Piece (with Keyser) *109*

Coup de Soleil, Le 112, 117, *131*
Dune Landscape with Plank Fence 120
Extensive Landscape with Ruined Castle and a Church, An 112, 116, *129*
Great Oak, The 114, 121
Hilly Wooded Landscape with Castle 114, *116-127*
Interior of the Old Church at Amsterdam, The 114
Jewish Cemetery, The 112, 118-19, *112*
Landscape with the Ruins of the Castle of Egmond 112-13
Panoramic View of the Amstel River Looking Towards Amsterdam 112-13
Pool Surrounded by Trees, A 112
Shore at Egmond-aan-Zee 113
Shore of the Zuider Zee near Naarden, The 114-15
Sun-dappled Trees at the Edge of a Stream 115
Sunlit Grain Field see Le Coup de Soleil
Sunlit Grain Field on the Banks of a Coast, A 125
Three Half-timbered Houses 115
Two Watermills and an Open Sluice 124
Vessels on a Breeze 123
View of Haarlem with the Bleaching Grounds 130
Village in Winter, A 113
Waterfall, A 127
Windmill and Cottages near a High Footbridge, A 114-15
Windmill at Wijk by Duurstede, The 126
Winter Landscape 112, 128
Ruysdael, Jacob Salonomsz 111
Landscape with Waterfall by a Cottage 110
Ruysdael, Salomon van 108
River Landscape 110

S

Sacrifice of Abraham, The (Caravaggio) 18, *26*
St John the Evangelist on the Island of Patmos (Velázquez) *50*
St John on Patmos (drawing, Pacheco after Velázquez) *44*
St Peter's Square (Bernini) *72*
Saraceni, Carlo, and Caravaggio 36-7
Seven Works of Mercy (Caravaggio) 37
Shore at Egmond-aan-Zee (Ruisdael) *113*
Shore of the Zuider Zee near Naarden, The (Ruisdael) *114-15*
Sketches of a Head (Van Dyck) *84-5*
Sofonisa Anguissola (sketch, Van Dyck) *80*
Soldiers, Playing Dice (Le Valentin) *36-7*
Spain 69, 72-3, 136
highest class of painter in 45
Spinners, The (Velázquez) *51*
Stadhuis, Amsterdam *137*
Stage of Welcome (Rubens) *106*
Still-Life (Caravaggio) *18, 21*
Still-Life (Zeuxiz) *21*
Study for a Head (drawing, Velázquez) *51*
Sun-dappled Trees at the Edge of a Stream (drawing, Ruisdael) *115*
Sunlit Grain Field (Ruisdael) *see Coup de Soleil, Le*
Sunlit Grain Field on the Banks of a Coast, A (Ruisdael) *125*
Supper at Emmaus (Caravaggio) 19, *22, 22-3, 28-9*
Surrender of Breda, The (Velázquez) 48, 52-3, *58-9*

T

tapestry manufacture:
I. van Ruisdael and 108
Rubens and 77
Van Dyck and 78
Terborch, Gerard *Ratification of the Treaty of Munster 136*
Terbrugghen, Hendrick 39, 141
Thomas Howard, 2nd Earl of Arundel and his Wife (Van Dyck) *77*
Three Half-timbered Houses (drawing, Ruisdael) *115*
Thirty Years War 69, 105, 136
Thornhill, Sir James 141
Titian 21, 51, 79, 80, 82
Pope Paul III 52
Tommasoni, Ranuccio 16
Triple Portrait of a Jeweller (Lotto) *87*
Two Watermills and an Open Sluice (Ruisdael) *124*

V

Valdés Leal, Juan de 141
Van Dyck, Anthony *9, 75*
and Anguissola *80*
in Antwerp 79, 81
apprenticeship 76
assistants 76
and backgrounds 82, 83
collaboration with Rubens *76-7*
commissions 77, *77*, 79, *80*
death of 81
description of 78, 81
early success 77-8
engaged by Rubens 77
in England 81, 84
family 76, 79, 81
finances 78, 80
friends, in Italy *79*
in Genoa *77*, 78-9, 82-3
influence on English portraiture 82-5
influence of Italian art on 77-8, 83-4
Venetian artists 79, 80, 82
influence of Rubens 76, 78, *78, 79*
influence of Titian 79, 80, 82
influence of Veronese 79, 80
in Italy 80, *80*
key dates 76
and landscape *79*, 82
last years 81
and line 84-5
in London 80-81
marriage 81
mistress *78*, 81
most productive period 79
and painters' guild 76
in Palermo *80*
in Paris 81
patrons 79-80
posts 79-81
and 'props' 84
sitters 83, 85
sketchbooks, of Italy 79, 80, *80*
studio 76, 84
style 78, 82, 84
subjects 79
and tapestry design 78
trademarks 84
and watercolour *79*
works by:
Character studies 84-5
Charles I on Horseback with Seigneur de St Antoine 92
Charles I in Three Positions 86, 87, 94-5
Christ Crowned with Thorns 88
Cupid and Psyche 98
Emperor Theodosius Refused Entry into Milan Cathedral, The 79
Five Children of Charles I 83, *96-7*
François Langlois 82-3
Henrietta Maria 87, 101
Lady Elizabeth Thimbleby and Dorothy, Viscountess Andover 99
Lomellini Family, The 82, 83
Lord John and Lord Bernard Stuart 84
Louis and Rupert of the Rhine 102-103
Lucas and Cornelis de Wael (copy, Hollar) *79*
Marchesa Elena Grimaldi 78, *82*, 83
Margaret Lemon 78
Marie de Raet 91
Mary Ruthven 81
Nicholas Lancier 80
Pembroke Family, The 84
Philippe le Roy, Seigneur de Ravels 90
Prince William of Orange and Princess Mary Stuart 83
Queen Henrietta Maria with her Dwarf Sir Jeffrey Hudson 93
Rest on the Flight into Egypt, The 89
Rinaldo and Armida 79, *81*
self-portraits *75, 76*
Sketches of a Head 84-5
Thomas Howard, 2nd Earl of Arundel and his Wife 77
Van Dyck, Frans 76
Velázquez, Antonio 49
Velázquez, Diego Rodríguez de Silva y *9, 43*
and Accademia di San Luca 49
apprenticeship 44-5
birthplace *44*
bodegones 50-51
and characterization 52-3
commissions, from Philip IV 46
death of 49
early training 44
and the Escorial *46, 47*
family 44, 45
grandchildren *48*
influence of Renaissance 48
influence of Titian 51
in Italy *46*, 47-9
key dates 44
in Madrid *45*, 45-7
marriage 45
medal of merit *48*
models, wife as? 45, *45*
most fruitful period 48-9
and Philip IV 46-7
and Pope Innocent X *48*
posts 46-7, 49
practice at portraits 50
pupils 53
pupil, outstanding 48
and Ribera 47-8
in Rome *46*, 49
royal favours 46-7
and Rubens 47, *47*
sitters, and 'inner life' of 50-53
speed of working 50
studio 53
style, subtlety of 50
subjects 48, 50-52
technique 52, *53*
trademarks 53
working methods 53
works: dating 50
total ouput 50
works by:
Adoration of the Magi, The 45, *45*
Artist's Family, The 48
Boar Hunt 68-9
Buffoon Juan de Calabazas, The 52, *53*
Court Fool 'El Primo', The 60
Court Fool Sebastián de Morra, The 61
Expulsion of the Moriscos, The 46
Forge of Vulcan, The 48
Gongora, Luis de 45, 46
Guzman, Gaspar de, Count of Olivares 68
Immaculate Conception, The 51, *55*
Infanta Margarita, The 54
Infanta Margarita in Blue, The 67
Innocent X 53, *65*
Isabel of Bourbon (with Jan Brueghel) *69*
Joseph's Coat 48
Juan de Pareja 64
Meninas, Las 49, 53, 54, *54-5, 66*
Old Woman Frying Eggs 50
Philip IV 46, *51, 68*
Prince Baltasar Carlos 70
Prince Philip Prosper 53
Rokeby Venus, The 50, *62-3*
St John the Evangelist on the Island of Patmos 44, 50
Spinners, The 51
Study for a Head 51
Surrender of Breda, The 48, 52-3, *58-9*
Villa Medici 47
Waterseller of Seville, The 51, *57*
Velázquez, Francisca 45, 48
Velázquez, Ignacia 45
Velde, Esaias van de 108, 112
Veronese 79, 80
Vessels in a Breeze (Ruisdael) *123*
Victorious Cupid (Caravaggio) 13, *19*
View of Haarlem with the Bleaching Grounds (Ruisdael) *130*
Villa Medici (oil sketch, Velázquez) *47*
Village in Winter, A (Ruisdael) *113*
Vroom, Cornelis *108-109*
Landscape with a River by a Wood 108-109

W

watercolour: Van Dyck and *79*
Waterfall, A (Ruisdael) *127*
Water-mill at Gillingham (Constable) *116*
Waterseller of Seville, The (Velázquez) 51, *57*
Windmill and Cottages near a High Footbridge, A (drawing, Ruisdael) *114-15*
Windmill at Wijk bij Duurstede, The (Ruisdael) *126*
Winter Landscape (Ruisdael) 112, *128*

Z

Zeuxis *21*
Zurburan, Francisco 141